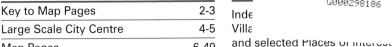

A-Z EX

G000298186

CONTEN

Key to Map Pages	2-3
Large Scale City Centre	4-5
Map Pages	6-49

Inde
Villa
and selected Places of interest

REFERENCE

Motorway	**M5**
A Road	A30
B Road	B3212
Dual Carriageway	
One-way Street Traffic flow on A Roads is also indicated by a heavy line on the driver's left.	
Road Under Construction Opening dates are correct at the time of publication.	
Proposed Road	
Restricted Access	
Pedestrianized Road	
Track / Footpath	
Residential Walkway	
Railway	Station / Tunnel Level Crossing
Built-up Area	
Local Authority Boundary	
Posttown Boundary	
Postcode Boundary (within Posttown)	

Map Continuation	**14**	Large Scale City Centre	**4**

Airport	✈

Car Park (selected)	**P**
Church or Chapel	†
City Wall (large scale only)	ЛЛЛ
Cycleway (selected)	
Fire Station	■
Hospital	**H**
House Numbers A & B Roads only	13 ... 8
Information Centre	**i**
National Grid Reference	³75
Park & Ride	Sowton **P+R**
Police Station	▲
Post Office	★
Safety Camera with Speed Limit Fixed cameras and long term road works cameras. Symbols do not indicate camera direction.	**(30)**
Toilet: without facilities for the Disabled with facilities for the Disabled	▽ ▽
Educational Establishment	▢
Hospital or Healthcare Building	▢
Industrial Building	▢
Leisure or Recreational Facility	▢
Place of Interest	▢
Public Building	▢
Shopping Centre or Market	▢
Other Selected Buildings	▢

SCALE

Map Pages 6-45	1:15,840		Map Pages 4-5	1:7,920

0	¼	½ Mile

0	250	500	750 Metres

4 inches (10.16 cm) to 1 mile 6.31 cm to 1 km

0	⅛	¼ Mile

0	100	200	300	400 Metres

8 inches (20.32cm) to 1 mile 12.63 cm to 1 km

Copyright of Geographers' A-Z Map Company Limited

Fairfield Road, Borough Green, Sevenoaks, Kent TN15 8PP
Telephone: 01732 781000 (Enquiries & Trade Sales)
01732 783422 (Retail Sales)

www.az.co.uk
Copyright © Geographers' A-Z Map Co. Ltd.
Edition 6   2013

 Ordnance Survey This product includes mapping data licensed
from Ordnance Survey® with the permission of
the Controller of Her Majesty's Stationery Office.

© Crown Copyright 2012. All rights reserved. Licence number 100017302
Safety camera information supplied by www.PocketGPSWorld.com
Speed Camera Location Database Copyright 2012 © PocketGPSWorld.com

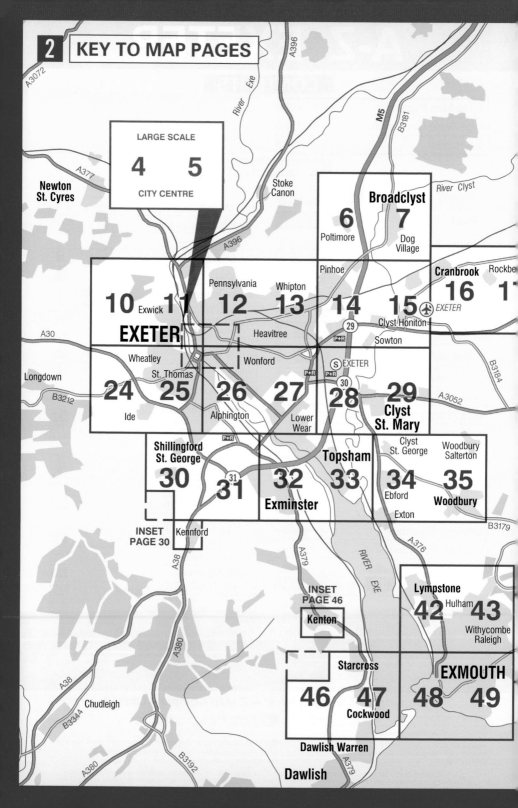

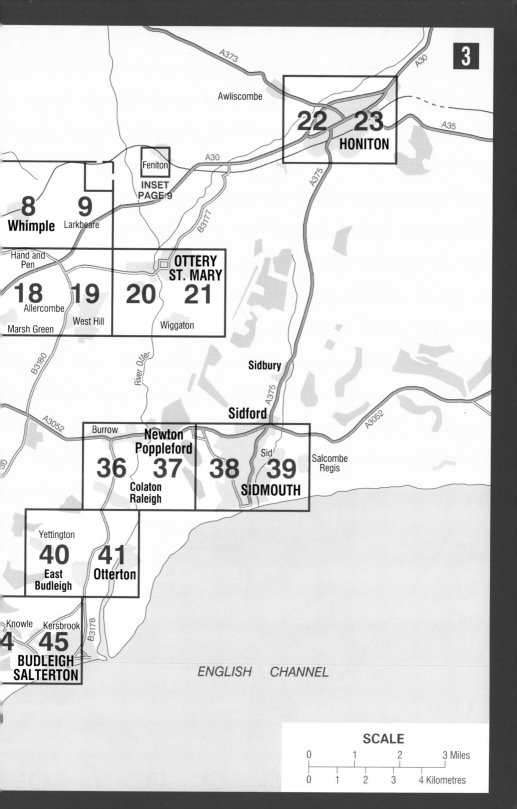

3

Awliscombe

22 **23**
HONITON

Feniton
INSET PAGE 9

8 **9**
Whimple Larkbeare

Hand and Pen

18 **19** **20** **21**
Allercombe

West Hill

Marsh Green

Wiggaton

OTTERY ST. MARY

River Otter

Sidbury

Sidford

Burrow

Newton Poppleford

36 **37** **38** **39**
Colaton Raleigh **SIDMOUTH**

Sid

Salcombe Regis

Yettington

40 **41**
East Budleigh **Otterton**

Knowle Kersbrook

4 **45**
BUDLEIGH SALTERTON

ENGLISH CHANNEL

SCALE

0   1   2   3 Miles

0   1   2   3   4 Kilometres

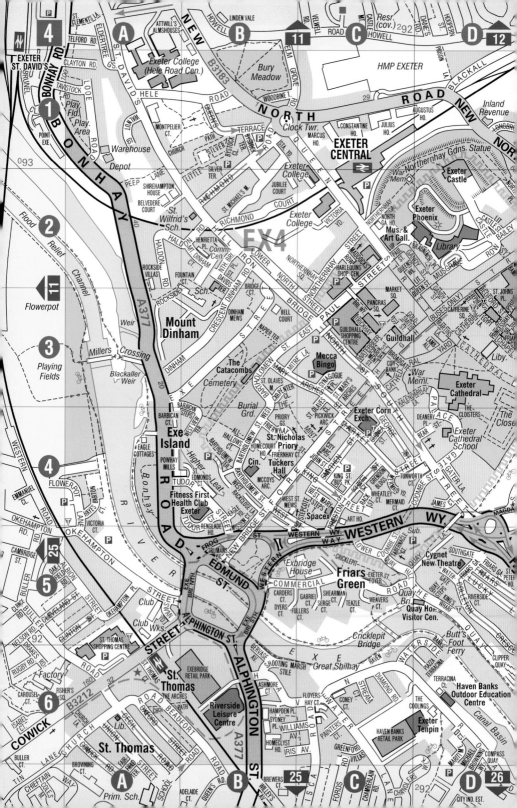

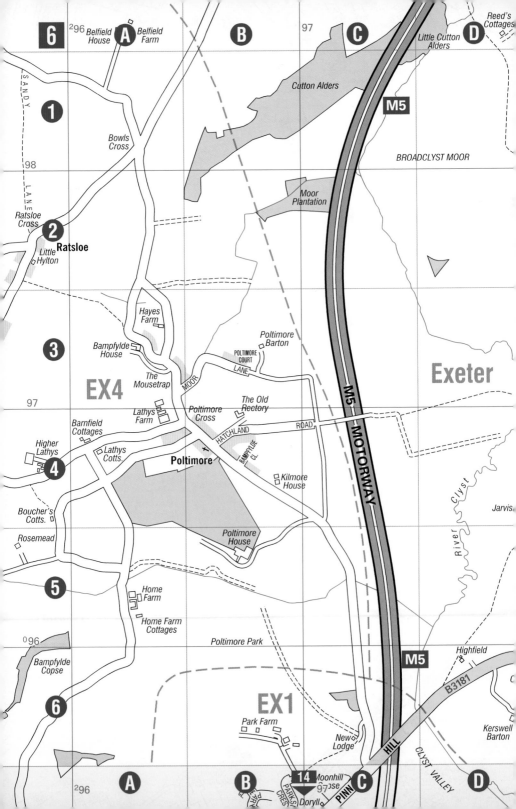

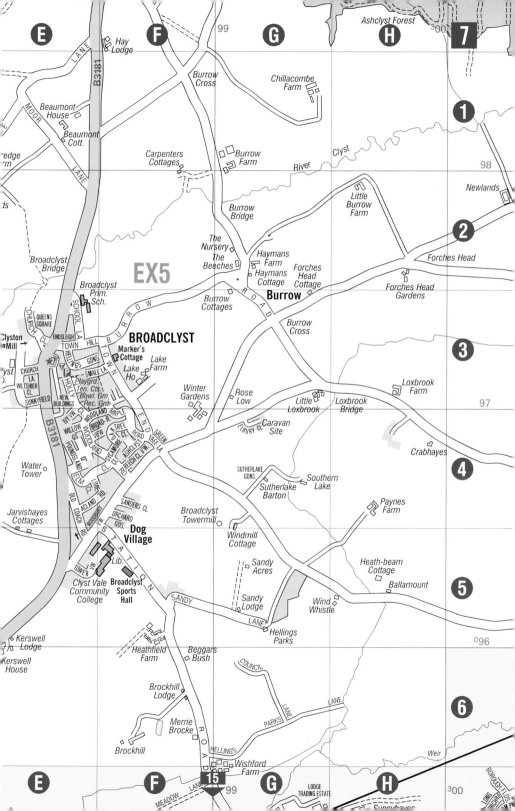

E **F** SILVERLEA COTTAGES MOORHAYES CT.

G Sherwood Farm 09

H Spts. Grd. 310 **9**

CLOSE EN MOUNT VIEW HIGH VW. Westlades Lismore

ST. ANDREW'S CL. FARM WY. AGLAND PK. Sch ROAD

STATION YORK RD. WELLS MOUNT WARWICK CL. COVENTRY CL. Hall **1**

Feniton EXETER FENITON GARDENS

FENITON WICHISTER CL. SALISBURY CL. BATH CL.

Long Park THE SIGNALS CRES. SALISBURY CL.

Honiton OTTERY MONTON GREENACRES CL. ROAD LANE 099

New Barn Sweethams ROAD GREEN **2**

EX14

INSET

Talaton Farm The Moor

Springfield Farm Three Corner Copse **3**

Larkbeare Farm Larkbeare Cross **Larkbeare** LARKBEARE

kbeare Court

Big Wood **4**

L A N E AVENUE

Loosemore Common 97

Holly Ball Larkbeare Brake **Ottery St. Mary** **5**

A30 **EX11**

R O A D Straightway Head Farm Birdcage Copse Lower Pitt Copse

Higher Pitt Copse **6**

raightway Head avan rk Birdcage Ledge Copse 096

BIRDCAGE

low Fm. **E** **F** **19** 07 **G** Meadow Lake The Green **H** OTTERY WOOD 08

LANE

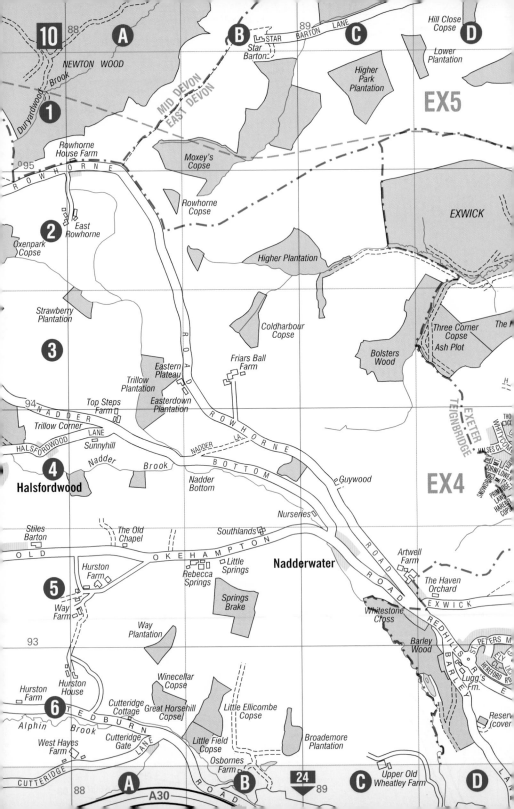

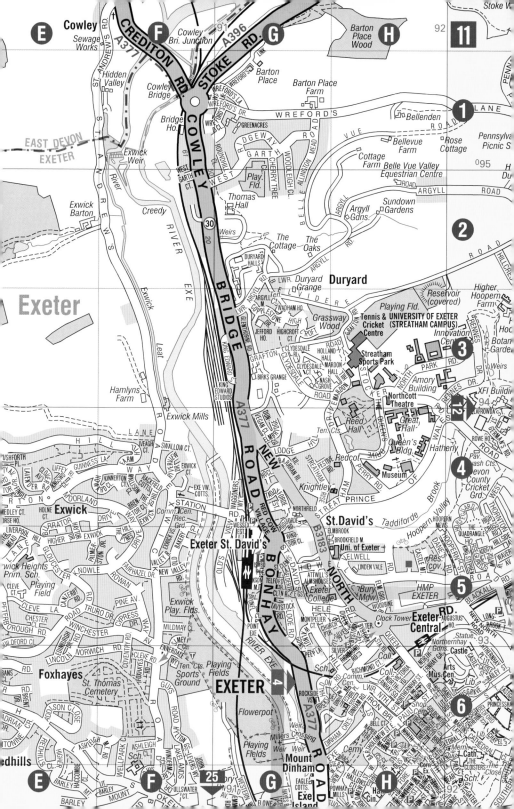

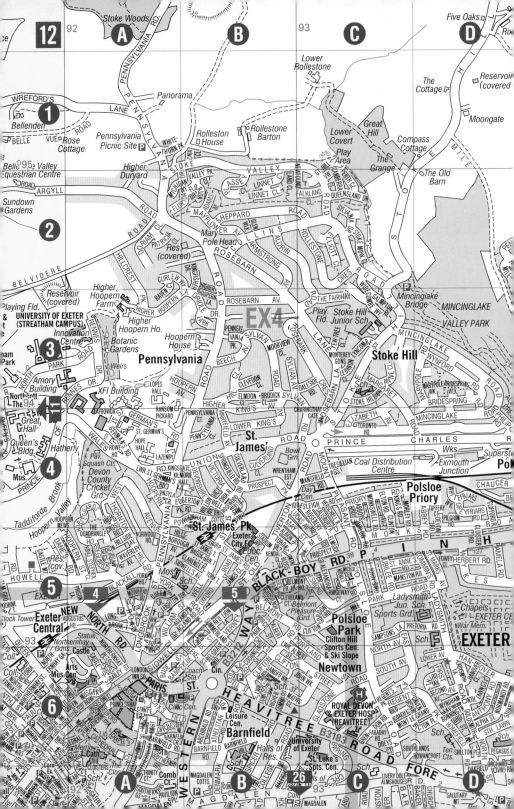

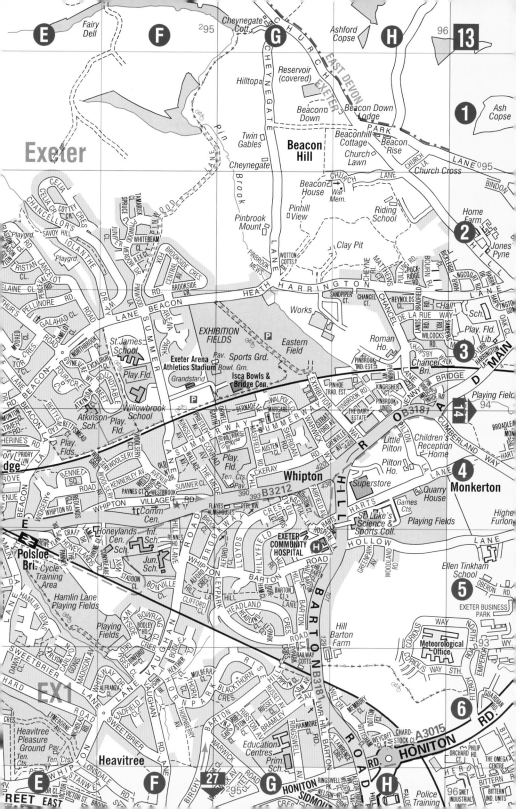

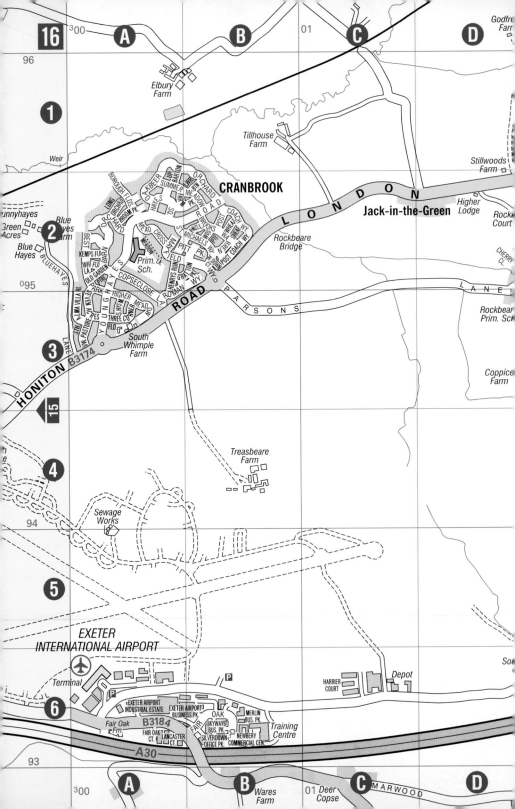

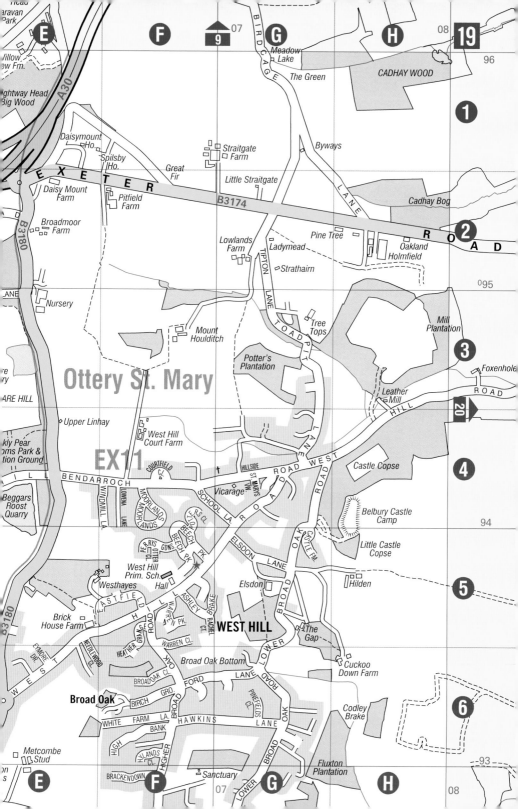

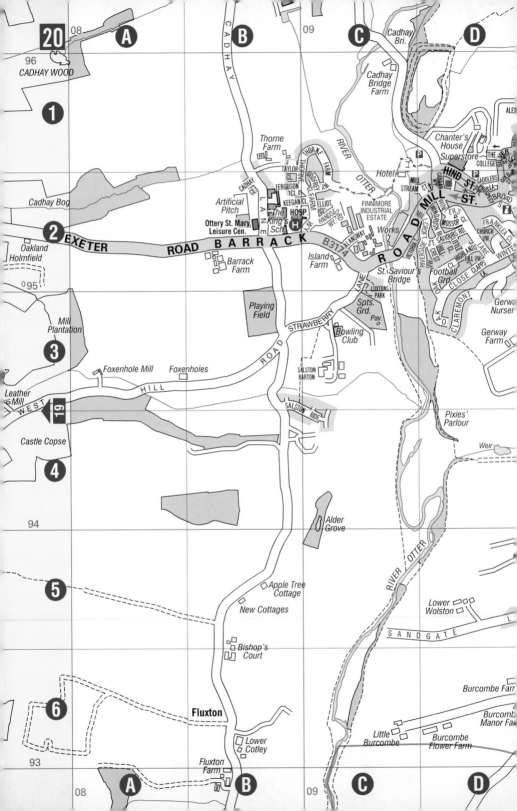

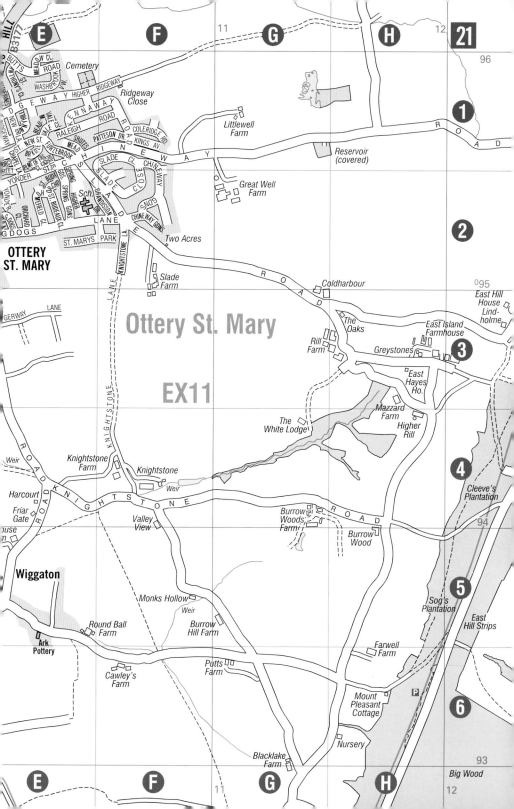

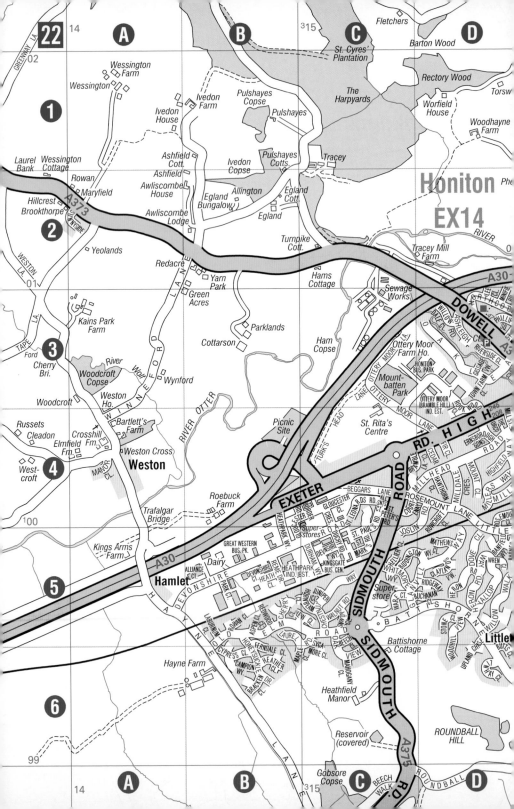

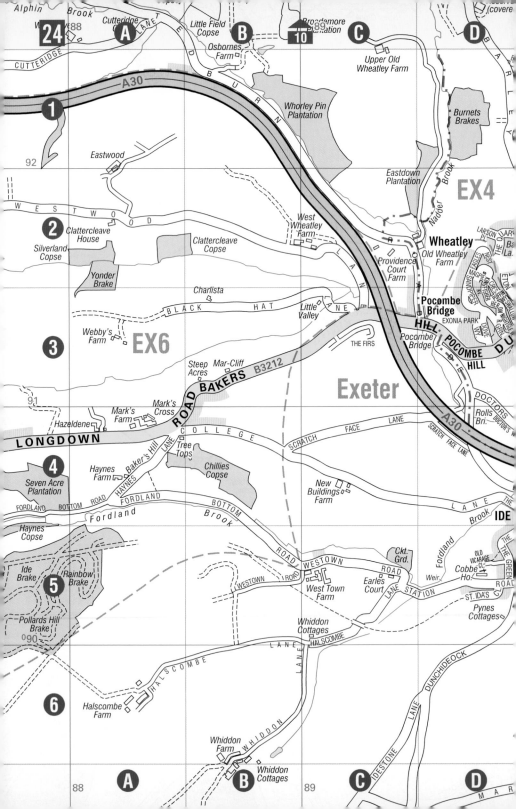

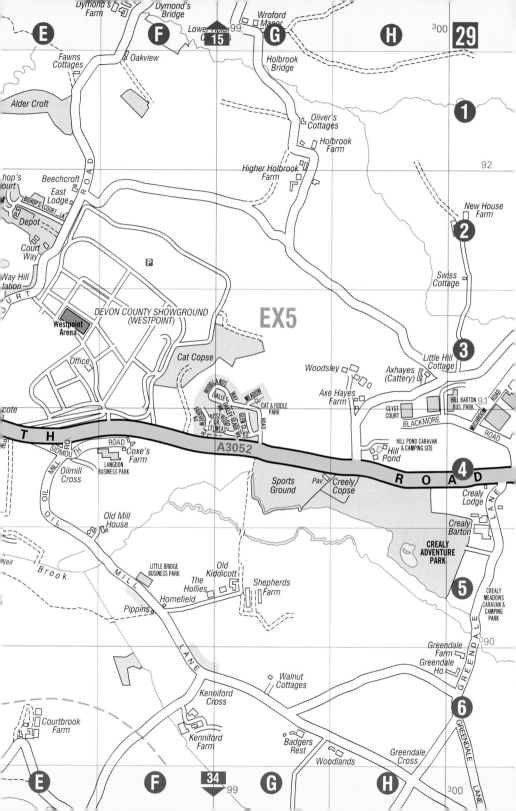

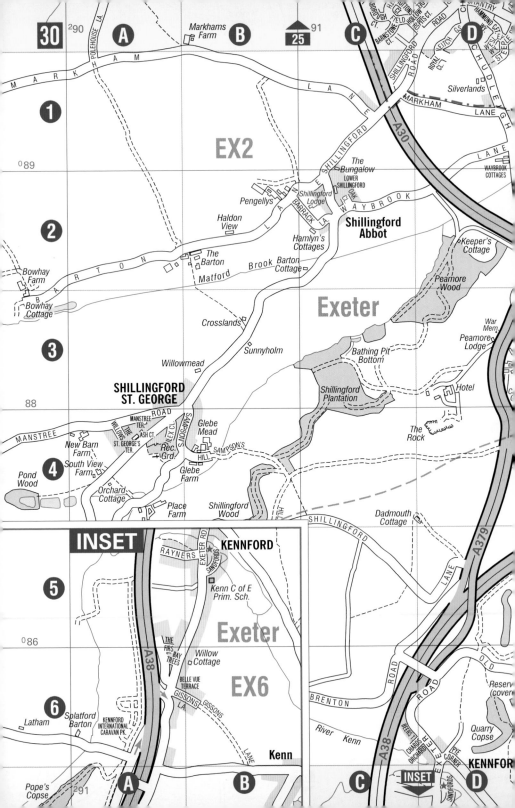

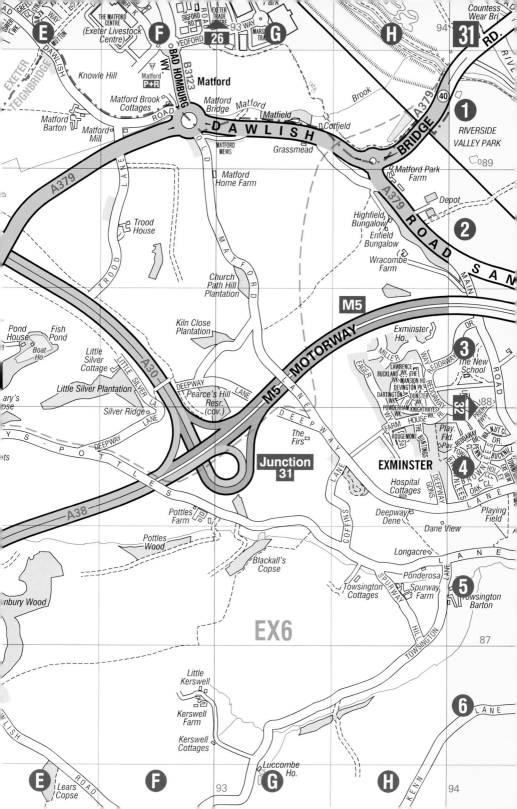

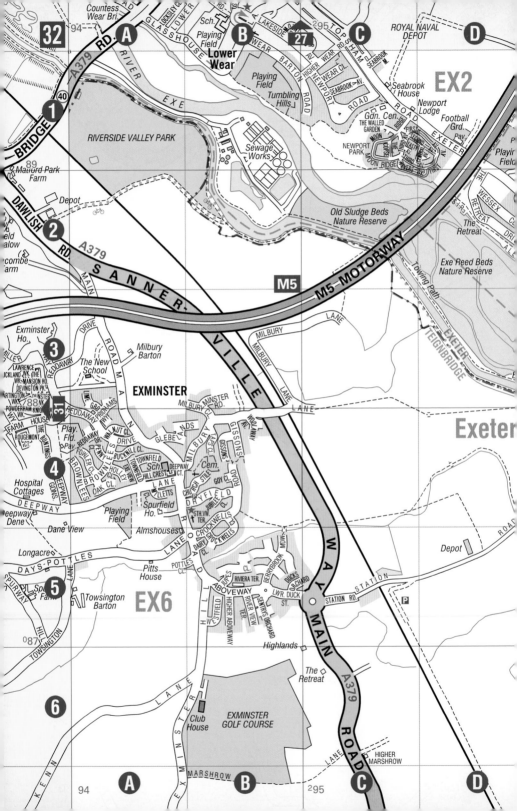

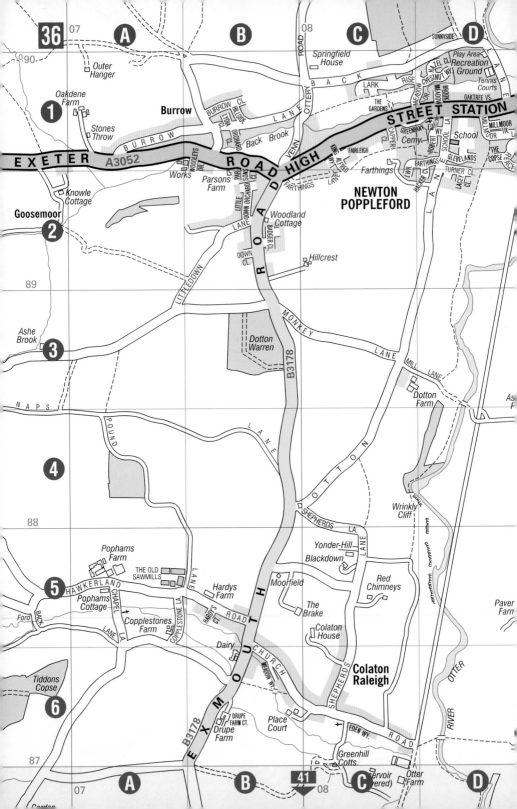

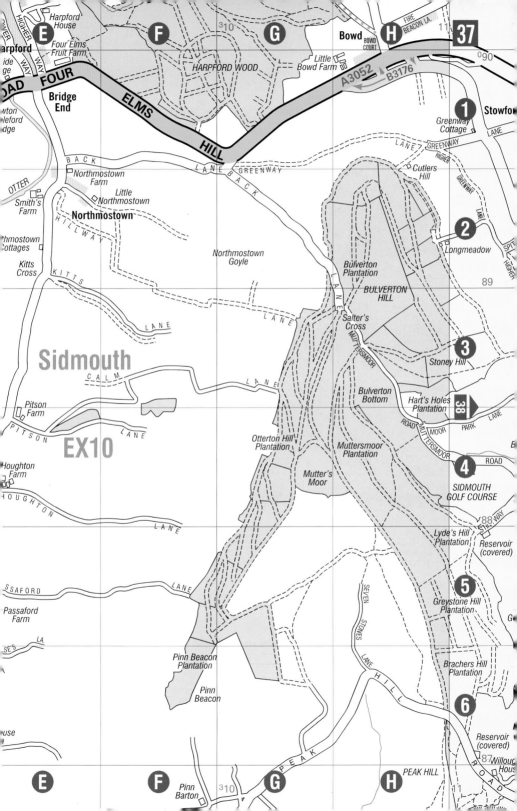

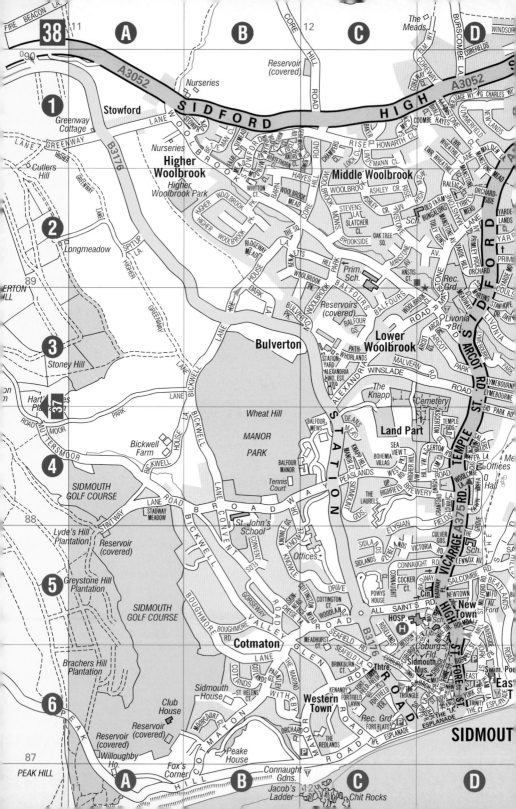

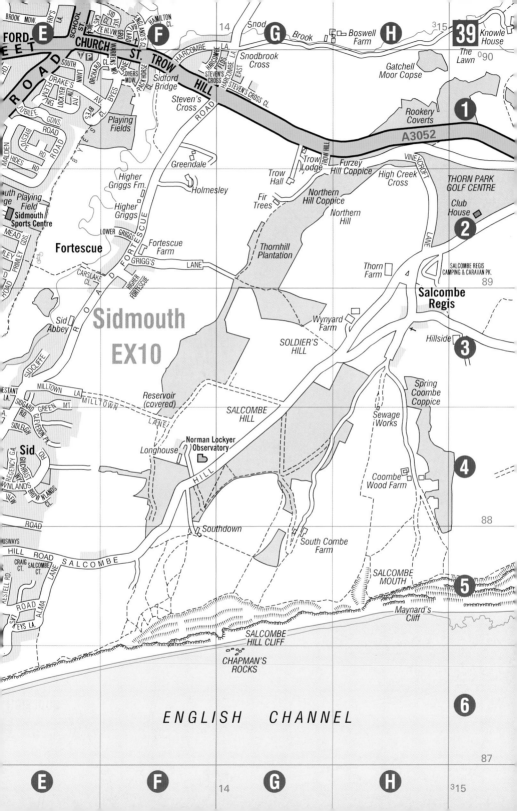

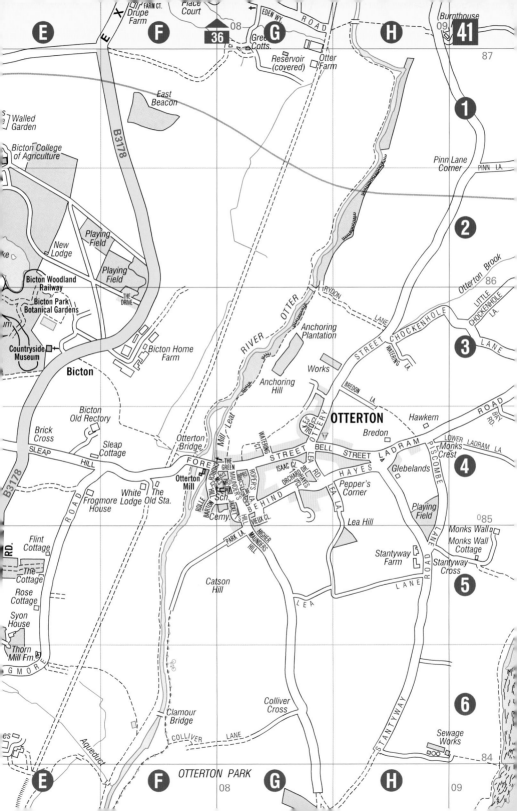

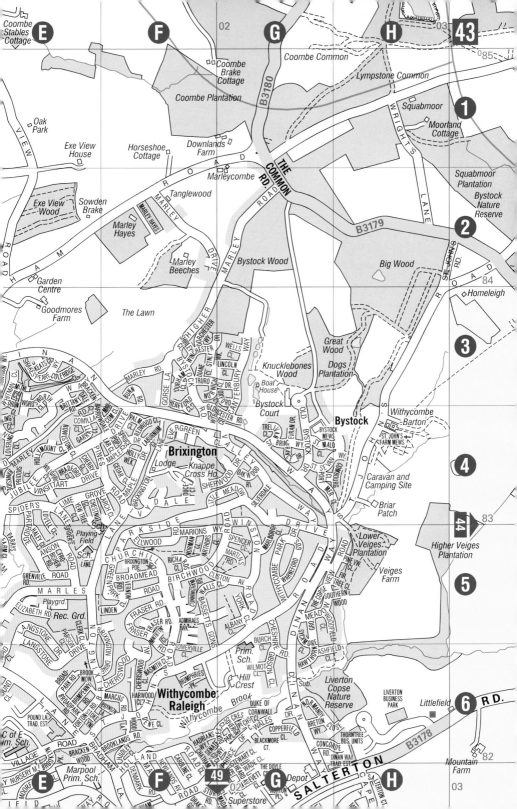

E Government Offs.
F Jetty
98
Starcross Sand
G
H
99
82

Starcross

STAPLACE
LONGFIELD EST.
COURTENAY
BONHAY CL.
 OLD EST.
PECK CT.
HENS
BARLEY COOMB.
WALK
BRICKYARD

STARCROSS

worthy
m

Staplake

OLD
LAKE
LANE

Old Staplake
Farm

HILL

LANE

Spinacre

Exeter

EX6

Southbrook

oon
ges

ROAD

PEACOCK PL.
Wks.
BONHAY R.
WELL ST.
SECOMBE CR.
A379
DRAW ST.
DREW'S
Sch
WARBORO RD.
COOKSONS RD.
CORAM
CHURCHTON
BRUNEL RD.
PARKER'S RD.
SWAN RD.
NEW
CHURCH ST.
WESTERN
HAMI
GRO.
GENERALS
GENERALS CL.

ROYAL WY.
ELM DR.
ALEX.
ANDRA W.
ST.
ROYAL DR.
COUNTISS
BISHOPS CL.
COUNTISS

Play.
Fld.

THE STRAND

Fishing &
Cruising Club
Jetty

STARCROSS

Club
Ho.

Oak Meadow
Golf Course

1

2
Little Bull
Hill
Shelly Bank
Point 81e

Exe
Sailing Clu
SCHOONER
HALYARDS
WINDJAMMER CT.
LEEWARD CT.
WINDWARD CT.
S. MADISON
WHARF
REG

3

ROAD

COFTON
RD.
VICARAGE
Sch.

Middlewood

WESTWOOD

COFTON HILL
HILL

twood

Cockwood

SCHOOL HILL
R'Y CR.
COFTON
CL.

48

Pie

Foot Ferry
(Summer Only)

4

Exe Estuary
Local Nature Reserve
080

Eastdon
Plantation

ORCHARD

Eastdon

Blencathra

Lodge

EASTDON
WOOD

Eastdon
House

Oakleigh

WARREN LANE

RIVER EXE
TEIGNBRIDGE
EAST DEVON

5

WARREN
GOLF COURSE
Dawlish Warren
National Nature Reserve

6

79

DAWLISH
SANDS
HOLIDAY PARK

WELCOME FAMILY
HOLIDAY PARK

SHERWELLS
CL.

MELLIN
WAY

ROAD

LANE

E
F
G
H

98
Club
House
Visitor
Centre
99

INDEX

Including Streets, Places & Areas, Hospitals etc., Industrial Estates,
Selected Flats & Walkways, Service Areas, Stations and Selected Places of Interest.

HOW TO USE THIS INDEX

1. Each street name is followed by its Postcode District, then by its Locality abbreviation(s) and then by its map reference;
   e.g. **Alexandria Rd.** EX10: Sidm . . . .3C **38** is in the EX10 Postcode District and the Sidmouth Locality and is to be found
   in square 3C on page **38**. The page number is shown in bold type.

2. A strict alphabetical order is followed in which Av., Rd., St., etc. (though abbreviated) are read in full and as part of the street name;
   e.g. **Clay La.** appears after **Claylands Vw.** but before **Clayton Rd.**

3. Streets and a selection of flats and walkways that cannot be shown on the mapping, appear in the index with the thoroughfare to
   which they are connected shown in brackets; e.g. **Admiral Vernon Ct.** *EX2: Alph* . . . .6H **25** *(off Chudleigh Rd.)*

4. Addresses that are in more than one part are referred to as not continuous.

5. Places and areas are shown in the index in BLUE TYPE and the map reference is to the actual map square in which the
   town centre or area is located and not to the place name shown on the map; e.g. **BUDLEIGH SALTERTON** 5G **45**

6. An example of a selected place of interest is Countryside Mus. 3E **41**

7. An example of a station is **Digby & Sowton Station (Rail)** . . . .2A **28**, also included is **Park & Ride**.
   e.g. **Honiton Road (Park & Ride)** 6A **14**

8. Service Areas are shown in the index in BOLD CAPITAL TYPE; e.g. **EXETER SERVICE AREA** 2B **28**

9. An example of a Hospital, Hospice or selected Healthcare facility is BUDLEIGH SALTERTON HOSPITAL 4H **45**

10. Map references for entries that appear on large scale pages **4** & **5** are shown first, with small scale map references shown in brackets;
    e.g. **Alphington St.** EX2: Exe 5B **4** (1H **25**)

GENERAL ABBREVIATIONS

All. : Alley	**Gdns.** : Gardens	**Pde.** : Parade
Arc. : Arcade	**Gth.** : Garth	**Pk.** : Park
Av. : Avenue	**Ga.** : Gate	**Pas.** : Passage
Bri. : Bridge	**Gt.** : Great	**Pl.** : Place
Bldgs. : Buildings	**Grn.** : Green	**Ri.** : Rise
Bungs. : Bungalows	**Gro.** : Grove	**Rd.** : Road
Bus. : Business	**Hgts.** : Heights	**Shop.** : Shopping
Cen. : Centre	**Ho.** : House	**Sth.** : South
Chu. : Church	**Ind.** : Industrial	**Sq.** : Square
Cl. : Close	**Info.** : Information	**St.** : Street
Cnr. : Corner	**Intl.** : International	**Ter.** : Terrace
Cott. : Cottage	**La.** : Lane	**Trad.** : Trading
Cotts. : Cottages	**Lit.** : Little	**Up.** : Upper
Ct. : Court	**Lwr.** : Lower	**Va.** : Vale
Cres. : Crescent	**Mnr.** : Manor	**Vw.** : View
Cft. : Croft	**Mans.** : Mansions	**Vs.** : Villas
Dr. : Drive	**Mdw.** : Meadow	**Vis.** : Visitors
E. : East	**Mdws.** : Meadows	**Wlk.** : Walk
Est. : Estate	**M.** : Mews	**W.** : West
Fld. : Field	**Mt.** : Mount	**Yd.** : Yard
Flds. : Fields	**Mus.** : Museum	
Gdn. : Garden	**Nth.** : North	

LOCALITY ABBREVIATIONS

Alph : **Alphington**	Daw W : **Dawlish Warren**	Kenton : **Kenton**
Awli : **Awliscombe**	E Bud : **East Budleigh**	Know : **Knowle**
Ayle : **Aylesbeare**	E'don : **Eastdon**	Lark : **Larkbeare**
Bic : **Bicton**	Ebf : **Ebford**	L'ham : **Littleham**
Bowd : **Bowd**	Exe : **Exeter**	Long : **Longdown**
Broadc : **Broadclyst**	Exmin : **Exminster**	Lymp : **Lympstone**
Bud S : **Budleigh Salterton**	Exmth : **Exmouth**	Mar B : **Marsh Barton**
Clyst H : **Clyst Honiton**	Exton : **Exton**	Mar G : **Marsh Green**
Clyst G : **Clyst St George**	Fen : **Feniton**	Matf : **Matford**
Clyst M : **Clyst St Mary**	Gitt : **Gittisham**	Monk : **Monkton**
Cockw : **Cockwood**	Hals : **Halsfordwood**	Nad : **Nadderwater**
Col R : **Colaton Raleigh**	Harp : **Harpford**	New P : **Newton Poppleford**
Com R : **Combe Raleigh**	Heav : **Heavitree**	N'town : **Northmostown**
Coom : **Coombelake**	High M : **Higher Metcombe**	Offw : **Offwell**
Cou W : **Countess Wear**	Hon : **Honiton**	Ott'n : **Otterton**
Cow : **Cowley**	Ide : **Ide**	Ott M : **Ottery St Mary**
Cranb : **Cranbrook**	Kenn : **Kenn**	Pin : **Pinhoe**
Daw : **Dawlish**	Kennf : **Kennford**	Polt : **Poltimore**

Column 1 (abbreviations key):

Rock : **Rockbeare**
Sal R : **Salcombe Regis**
San B : **Sandy Bay**
Shil A : **Shillingford Abbot**
Shil G : **Shillingford St George**
Sidb : **Sidbury**
Sidf : **Sidford**
Sidm : **Sidmouth**
Sow : **Sowton**

Column 2 (abbreviations key):

Star : **Starcross**
Stow : **Stowford**
Stre R : **Strete Ralegh**
Tala : **Talaton**
Top : **Topsham**
W Cly : **West Clyst**
W Hill : **West Hill**
Westo : **Weston**
Whim : **Whimple**

Column 3 (abbreviations key):

Whip : **Whipton**
White : **Whitestone**
Wigg : **Wiggaton**
Won : **Wonford**
Wood : **Woodbury**
Wood S : **Woodbury Salterton**
Yett : **Yettington**

A

Abbeville Cl. EX2: Exe 3C 26
Abbey Ct. EX2: Sow 1B 28
Abbey Rd. EX4: Exe 4D 12
Abbey Vw. EX10: Sidm 4E 39
Abbots Rd. EX4: Exe 4C 12
Aboveway EX6: Exmin 5B 32
Acland Pk. EX14: Fen 1H 9
Acland Rd. EX4: Exe 1F 5 (5B 12)
    EX5: Broadc 4E 7
Acland Ter. EX4: Exe 1F 5 (5A 12)
Addington Ct. EX4: Exe 5A 12
Addison Cl. EX4: Exe 6E 11
Addlepool Bus. Cen.
    EX3: Clyst G 2A 34
Adelaide Ct. EX2: Exe 6B 4
Admirals Ct. EX8: Exmth 3C 48
Admirals Wlk. EX8: Exmth 5F 43
Admiral Vernon Cl. EX2: Alph 6H 25
    (off Chudleigh Rd.)
Alansway EX11: Ott M 2C 20
A La Ronde 4C 42
Albany Cl. EX8: Exmth 5G 43
Alberta Cres. EX4: Exe 3D 12
Albert Pl. EX8: Exmth 3C 48
Albert St. EX1: Exe 1G 5 (5B 12)
Albion Ct. EX8: Exmth 3C 48
    (off Albion Pl.)
Albion Hill EX8: Exmth 2D 48
Albion Pl. EX4: Exe 5B 12
    EX8: Exmth 2C 48
Albion St. EX4: Exe 5A 4 (1G 25)
    EX8: Exmth 2C 48
Albion Ter. EX8: Exmth 3C 48
    (off Henrietta Rd.)
Aldborough Ct. EX8: Exmth 3E 49
Aldens Grn. EX2: Alph 6H 25
Aldens Rd. EX2: Alph 6H 25
Alderson Dr. EX2: Sow 1H 27
Aldrin Rd. EX4: Exe 2B 12
Alexander Pl. EX11: Ott M 1D 20
Alexander Wlk. EX2: Won 1H 27
Alexandra M. EX6: Star 1F 47
Alexandra Ter. EX4: Exe 1H 5 (5C 12)
    EX5: Broadc 2G 15
    EX6: Star 1F 47
    (off Royal Way)
    EX8: Exmth 3B 48
Alexandria Ind. Est. EX10: Sidm . . .3C 38
Alexandria Rd. EX10: Sidm 4D 38
Alford Cl. EX1: Whip 5G 13
Alford Cres. EX1: Whip 5F 13
Alfranza Cl. EX1: Heav 6F 13
Alice Templer Cl. EX2: Won 3D 26
ALLERCOMBE 4B 18
Allercombe Hill EX5: Rock 3C 18
Allercombe La. EX5: Rock 4B 18
ALLER GROVE 5D 8
Aller Va. Cl. EX2: Won 2F 27
Allhallows Ct. EX4: Exe 4B 4 (1H 25)
    EX14: Hon 3E 23
    (off Northcote La.)
Allhallows Museum of
    Lace & Local Antiquities 3E 23

Alliance Ct. EX14: Hon 5B 22
Allington Mead EX4: Exe 2G 11
All Saints Cl. EX9: E Bud 5D 40
All Saints Ct. EX14: Hon 4C 22
All Saint's Rd. EX10: Sidm 5C 38
Alma La. EX10: Sidm 5E 39
Alma Pl. EX2: Heav 1D 26
    (off Sivell Pl.)
Alma Villa Ri. EX5: Cranb 3A 16
Alpha Centre, The EX2: Sow 1B 28
Alpha St. EX1: Heav 6D 12
Alphin Brook Ct. EX2: Mar B 5A 26
Alphin Brook Rd. EX2: Mar B 5H 25
ALPHINGTON 5H 25
Alphington Rd. EX2: Exe 4H 25
Alphington Spur EX2: Exe 5G 25
Alphington St. EX2: Exe 5B 4 (1H 25)
Alston Ter. EX8: Exmth 3B 48
Altamira EX3: Top 3F 33
Ambassador Dr. EX1: Sow 5A 14
Amersham Ct. EX2: Won 2E 27
    (off Wonford St.)
Amity Pl. EX3: Top 4F 33
Amyatts Ter. EX10: Sidm 6D 38
    (off Church St.)
Andrew Cl. EX10: Sidm 1B 38
Angel M. EX14: Hon 3E 23
    (off Silver St.)
Anne Cl. EX4: Exe 3C 12
Anson Rd. EX8: Exmth 5E 43
Anstis Ct. EX10: Sidm 2C 38
Anthony Rd. EX1: Heav 6D 12
Antonine Cres. EX4: Exe 6E 11
Apple Cl. EX8: Exmth 4D 42
Apple Farm Grange EX2: Sow 3A 28
Applehayes EX8: Exmth 4E 49
Apple La. EX2: Sow 3A 28
April Cl. EX8: Exmth 4D 42
Arch, The EX5: Wood 5F 35
Arches, The EX2: Exe 6A 4
Archibald Rd. EX1: Exe 3F 5 (6B 12)
Arcot Gdns. EX10: Sidm 3D 38
Arcot Pk. EX10: Sidm 3D 38
Arcot Rd. EX10: Sidm 3D 38
Arden Cl. EX9: Bud S 5G 45
Ardenney Ct. EX8: Exmth 4E 49
Arena Pk. EX4: Whip 3F 13
Argus Cl. EX14: Hon 3F 23
Argyll M. EX4: Exe 3G 11
Argyll Rd. EX4: Exe 2H 11
Ark Pottery 5E 21
Armada Ct. EX3: Top 3F 33
Armstrong Av. EX4: Exe 2B 12
Armytage Rd. EX9: Bud S 3G 45
Art Ho. EX1: Exe 4C 4
Arthurs Cl. EX8: Exmth 5F 43
Arthur's Rd. EX4: Whip 3E 13
Artillery Ct. EX8: Exmth 3C 26
Arundel Cl. EX2: Alph 6H 25
Ascerton Cl. EX10: Sidm 4D 38
Ascerton Rd. EX10: Sidm 4D 38
Ashclyst Vw. EX5: Broadc 4F 7
Ash Ct. EX2: Shil G 4A 30
Ash Farm Cl. EX1: Pin 3B 14
Ashfield Cl. EX8: Exmth 6G 43
Ashford Rd. EX3: Top 3E 33

Ash Gro. EX8: Exmth 5D 42
Ash Leigh EX2: Alph 6G 25
Ashleigh Cl. EX4: Exe 6F 11
Ashleigh Mt. Rd. EX4: Exe 6E 11
Ashleigh Rd. EX8: Exmth 2D 48
    EX14: Hon 3D 22
Ashley Brake EX11: W Hill 5F 19
Ashley Cres. EX10: Sidm 2C 38
Ashley Ho. EX8: Exmth 3D 48
Ashmore Ct. EX2: Exe 6B 4
Ashton Rd. EX2: Mar B 4H 25
Ashwood Rd. EX2: Exe 3H 25
Aspen Cl. EX2: Won 2G 27
    EX14: Hon 5B 22
Athelstan Rd. EX1: Exe 3F 5 (6B 12)
Atkinson Cl. EX4: Whip 3E 13
Attwill's Almshouses
    EX4: Exe 1A 4 (5G 11)
Attwyll Av. EX2: Won 1E 27
Atwill-Kingdon Almshouses
    EX1: Exe 3H 5
Augustus Ho. EX4: Exe 1D 4 (5A 12)
Austen Cl. EX4: Whip 4G 13
Avalon Cl. EX4: Whip 2E 13
Avenue Mezidon-Canon EX14: Hon . .4F 23
Avocet Dr. EX3: Exton 6A 34
Avocet Rd. EX2: Sow 6B 14
Avondale Rd. EX2: Won 1E 27
    EX8: Exmth 1F 49
Axminster Rd. EX14: Hon 4G 23

B

Babblebrook M. EX1: Pin 4B 14
Back La. EX10: Col R 5A 36
    EX10: New P 1C 36
    EX10: N'town 1E 37
Badger Cl. EX2: Won 1H 27
    EX10: New P 2B 36
    EX14: Hon 2G 23
Bad Homburg Way
    EX2: Mar B, Matf 6B 26
Badon Cl. EX4: Whip 2E 13
Bagshot Av. EX2: Exe 3B 26
Bailey St. EX4: Exe 2D 4 (6A 12)
Baker Cl. EX10: Sidm 1C 38
Bakers Hill EX2: Exe 3B 24
    EX6: Long 3B 24
Baker St. EX2: Won 1D 26
Bakery La. EX8: Exmth 2C 48
Balfour Cl. EX14: Hon 4G 23
Balfour Gdns. EX10: Sidm 3C 38
Balfour Mnr. EX10: Sidm 4B 38
Balfour M. EX10: Sidm 4C 38
Balfours EX10: Sidm 2C 38
Ballard Gro. EX10: Sidf 1F 39
Ball's Farm Rd. EX2: Exe, Ide 4E 25
Balmoral Gdns. EX3: Top 3F 33
Bampfylde Cl. EX4: Polt 4B 6
Bampfylde La. EX1: Exe 2D 4
Bampfylde St. EX1: Exe 2E 5 (6A 12)
Banfield Way EX14: Hon 5D 22
Bankside EX8: Exmth 4E 43
Bapton Cl. EX8: Exmth 5D 42
Bapton La. EX8: Exmth 6D 42

Barbican Ct. EX4: Exe 4A **4**
Barbican Steps EX4: Exe 3B **4** (6H **11**)
Baring Ct. EX2: Exe 6E **5**
Baring Cres. EX1: Exe 4H **5** (6C **12**)
Baring Ter. EX2: Exe 6E **5** (2A **26**)
Barle Cl. EX2: Sow 2H **27**
Barleycorn EX5: Cranb 2B **16**
    (off Brooks Warren)
Barley Farm Rd. EX4: Exe 2E **25**
Barley La. EX4: Exe 6D **10**
Barley Mt. EX4: Exe 1E **25**
Barley Wlk. EX6: Star 1E **47**
Barnardo Rd. EX2: Exe 6E **5** (2B **26**)
Barnes Cl. EX14: Hon 5D **22**
BARNFIELD 3F **5** (6B **12**)
Barnfield Av. EX8: Exmth 2F **49**
Barnfield Cres. EX1: Exe 3E **5** (6A **12**)
Barnfield Hill EX1: Exe 3F **5** (6B **12**)
Barnfield Rd. EX1: Exe 3E **5** (6A **12**)
    (not continuous)
Barnfield Theatre 3E **5** (6A **12**)
Barn Hayes EX10: Sidm 2B **38**
Barn La. EX9: Bud S 3F **45**
Barn Orchard EX5: Cranb 2A **16**
Barnridge EX8: Lymp 2B **42**
Barns Rd. EX9: Bud S 4H **45**
Barnstone Ct. EX2: Alph 6G **25**
Barrack La. EX2: Shil A 2C **30**
Barrack Rd. EX2: Exe, Won 1C **26**
  EX11: Ott M 2B **20**
Barrington Mead *EX10: Sidm* 5D **38**
    (off Salcombe Rd.)
Barrowdale Cl. EX8: Exmth 4E **43**
Bartholomew St. E.
  EX4: Exe 3B **4** (6H **11**)
Bartholomew St. W.
  EX4: Exe 4B **4** (1H **25**)
Bartholomew Ter. EX4: Exe 4B **4**
Barton Cl. EX3: Exton 6A **34**
  EX10: Sidm 6C **38**
    (off The Triangle)
Barton Ct. EX1: Whip 5G **13**
  EX10: Sidm 6C **38**
    (off The Triangle)
Barton La. EX2: Shil A 2A **30**
Barton Lodge EX8: Exmth 3D **48**
Barton M. EX3: Exton 6A **34**
Barton Rd. EX2: Exe 2F **25**
Bartons, The *EX1: Heav* 1F **27**
    (off Honiton Rd.)
Bassetts Gdns. EX8: Exmth 5F **43**
Batavia Dr. EX2: Cou W 5H **27**
Bate Cl. EX2: Alph 5G **25**
Bath Cl. EX14: Fen 1H **9**
Bathern Rd. EX2: Sow 2H **27**
Bath Rd. EX8: Exmth 3C **48**
Battishorne Way EX14: Hon 5C **22**
Batt's La. EX11: Ott M 2D **20**
Baxter Cl. EX2: Sow 3H **27**
Bay Rd. EX9: Ott'n 4H **41**
Bay Trees EX6: Kennf 6A **30**
Bazley Sq. EX1: Pin 4A **14**
Beacon, The EX8: Exmth 3C **48**
Beacon Av. EX4: Whip 4D **12**
Beacon Heath EX4: Whip 3F **13**
BEACON HILL 1G **13**
Beacon Hill EX8: Exmth 3C **48**
Beacon La. EX4: Whip 3E **13**
Beacon Pl. EX8: Exmth 3C **48**
Bear La. EX9: Know 2E **45**
Bear St. EX1: Exe 4D **4** (1A **26**)
Beatlands Rd. EX10: Sidm 5D **38**
Beaufort Rd. EX2: Exe 6A **4** (2H **25**)
Beauvale Cl. EX11: Ott M 1E **21**
Beaworthy Cl. EX2: Exe 4G **25**
Bedford Ho. *EX1: Exe* 3D **4**
    (off Bedford St.)

Bedford Sq. EX10: Sidm 6D **38**
Bedford St. EX1: Exe 3D **4** (6A **12**)
Bedland's La. EX9: Bud S 3E **45**
Beech Av. EX4: Exe 3B **12**
Beech Cl. EX5: Broadc 4F **7**
  EX14: Hon 5C **22**
Beeches Cl. EX5: Wood 6F **35**
Beech Pk. EX11: W Hill 5F **19**
Beech Wlk. EX14: Gitt, Hon 6C **22**
Beechway EX8: Exmth 1D **48**
Beers Ter. EX6: Kennf 6C **30**
Beggars La. EX14: Hon 4C **22**
Behind Hayes EX9: Ott'n 4G **41**
Belgrave La. EX9: Bud S 5F **45**
Belgrave Rd. EX1: Exe 2F **5** (6B **12**)
Bell Ct. EX4: Exe 3B **4** (6H **11**)
Belle Isle Dr. EX2: Exe 2B **26**
Belle Vue EX6: Kenton 1A **46**
Belle Vue Rd. EX4: Exe 2G **11**
  EX8: Exmth 1C **48**
Belle Vue Ter. EX6: Kennf 6B **30**
Bell St. EX9: Ott'n 4G **41**
Belmont Ho. EX4: Exe 1G **5** (5B **12**)
Belmont Rd. EX1: Exe 1G **5** (5B **12**)
Belmont Ter. EX8: Exmth 6E **43**
Belvedere Cl. EX3: Top 2E **33**
Belvedere Ct. EX4: Exe 2A **4**
  EX10: Sidm 5D **38**
Belvedere Rd. EX8: Exmth 2C **48**
Belvidere Rd. EX4: Exe 3G **11**
Bendarroch Rd. EX11: W Hill 4E **19**
Bennett Cl. EX2: Alph 6G **25**
Bennetts Hill EX10: Sidm 2B **38**
Bennett Sq. EX4: Whip 4E **13**
Berkshire Dr. EX4: Exe 2E **25**
Bernadette Cl. EX4: Whip 3G **13**
Berrybrook Mdw. EX6: Exmin 5B **32**
Berry Cl. EX8: Exmth 1G **49**
Besley Ct. EX2: Mar B 3H **25**
Best Pk. EX5: Cranb 2A **16**
Betjeman Cl. EX10: Sidm 1B **38**
Betjeman Dr. EX8: Exmth 4E **43**
Betony Ri. EX2: Won 3G **27**
Bettysmead EX4: Whip 3E **13**
Bettysmead Ct. EX4: Whip 4E **13**
Beverley Cl. EX2: Won 2F **27**
Bhutan Cl. EX14: Hon 4F **23**
Bickleigh Cl. EX4: Pin 2H **13**
Bickwell Ho. La. EX10: Sidm 4A **38**
Bickwell La. EX10: Sidm 3B **38**
Bickwell Valley EX10: Sidm 5B **38**
BICTON .3E **41**
Bicton Park 2D **40**
Bicton Park Botanical Gdns. 3D **41**
Bicton Pl. EX1: Heav 6D **12**
  EX8: Exmth 3C **48**
Bicton St. EX8: Exmth 3C **48**
Bicton Vs. EX8: Exmth 3D **48**
Bicton Woodland Railway 2E **41**
Biddington Way EX14: Hon 5C **22**
Bidmead Cl. EX8: L'ham 2G **49**
Bill Douglas Centre, The 4H **11**
Bindon Rd. EX4: Pin 2A **14**
Binford Cl. EX1: Whip 6F **13**
Birch End EX5: Rock 3E **17**
Birch Gro. EX11: W Hill 6F **19**
Birch Rd. EX8: Lymp 2B **42**
Birchwood Rd. EX8: Exmth 5F **43**
Birchy Barton Hill EX1: Heav 1F **27**
Birdcage La. EX11: Ott M 6F **9**
Bird Cl. EX1: Pin 3A **14**
Birkett Cl. EX2: Won 2G **27**
Birks Grange EX4: Exe 2A **4**
Bishops Cl. EX6: Star 1F **47**
BISHOPS CLYST 3C **28**
Bishops Ct. Ind. Est. EX2: Sow 2A **28**
Bishop's Ct. La. EX5: Clyst M 2E **29**

Bishop's Ct. Rd.
  EX5: Clyst H, Clyst M 3C **28**
Bishop Westall Ho. *EX2: Exe* 5D **4**
    (off Good Shepherd Dr.)
Bishop Westall Rd. EX2: Cou W 4E **27**
Bittern Ind. Units EX2: Sow 1A **28**
Bittern Rd. EX2: Sow 6A **14**
Blackall Rd. EX4: Exe 1D **4** (5A **12**)
Blackboy Rd. EX4: Exe 1G **5** (5B **12**)
Black Hat La. EX6: Long 3A **24**
BLACKHORSE 4E **15**
Blackhorse La. EX5: Clyst H 4B **14**
Black Lion Ct. EX14: Hon 3E **23**
Blackmore Ct. EX8: Exmth 6G **43**
Blackmore Dr. EX10: Sidm 5D **38**
Blackmore M. EX2: Won 2G **27**
Blackmore Rd. EX5: Clyst M 4H **29**
Blackmore Theatre 3C **5**
Blackmore Vw. *EX10: Sidm* 5D **38**
    (off May Ter.)
Blackthorn Cl. EX10: Sidm 1B **38**
  EX14: Hon 5E **23**
Blackthorn Cres. EX1: Whip 6G **13**
Blair Atholl EX8: Exmth 4E **49**
Blakeslee Dr. EX2: Cou W 5H **27**
Blenheim Ct. EX2: Matf 5A **26**
Blenheim Rd. EX2: Alph 4H **25**
Blueberry Downs EX9: Bud S 4H **45**
Blueboy La. *EX1: Exe* 2E **5**
    (off Dix's Field)
Blue Boy Sq. EX1: Exe 2E **5**
Blue Cedar Ct. EX8: Exmth 3D **48**
Bluehayes La. EX5: Broadc 1H **15**
Boarden Barn EX8: Exmth 3D **48**
Bodley Cl. EX1: Whip 6F **13**
Bodley Ho. EX1: Whip 5F **13**
Bogmoor La. EX5: Whim 2A **8**
Bohemia Vs. EX10: Sidm 4C **38**
Bond's La. EX5: Wood, Wood S 4E **35**
Bonfire La. EX5: Wood 5F **35**
Bonhay Cl. EX6: Star 1F **47**
Bonhay Ho. *EX4: Exe* 1A **4**
    (off Bonhay Rd.)
Bonhay Rd. EX4: Exe 1A **4** (5G **11**)
  EX6: Star 1F **47**
Bonnington Gro. EX1: Heav 6D **12**
Bonville Cl. EX1: Whip 5F **13**
Booth Way EX8: Exmth 5D **42**
Border Rd. EX14: Hon 4C **22**
Borough Flds. EX5: Cranb 2A **16**
Boucher Rd. EX9: Bud S 4H **45**
Boucher Way EX9: Bud S 4H **45**
Boughmore La. EX10: Sidm 5B **38**
Boughmore Rd. EX10: Sidm 5B **38**
Bourn Ri. EX4: Pin 2H **13**
Bovemoor's La. EX2: Won 1D **26**
BOWD 1H **37**
Bowd Ct. EX10: Bowd 1H **37**
Bowe Ct. EX1: Exe 1H **5**
Bowhay La. EX4: Exe 1D **24**
Bowhill 2F **25**
Bowling Grn. La. EX14: Hon 4E **23**
Bowling Green Marsh Bird Sanctuary
. . . . .5G **33**
Bowling Green Marsh Nature Reserve
. . . . .4G **33**
Bowling Grn. Rd. EX3: Top 4G **33**
Bowring Cl. EX1: Whip 5F **13**
Boyne Rd. EX9: Bud S 3G **45**
Bracken Cl. EX14: Hon 6B **22**
Brackendale EX8: Exmth 3E **43**
Brackendown EX11: W Hill 6F **19**
Brackenwood EX2: Exmth 6E **43**
Bradfield Rd. EX4: Pin 3H **13**
Bradford Cl. EX8: Exmth 4E **43**
Bradham Ct. EX8: Exmth 1F **49**
Bradham La. EX8: Exmth 6E **43**

Bradman Way EX2: Mar B 4H 25
Bradninch Pl. EX4: Exe 2D 4
Bramble Cl. EX9: Bud S 4H 45
    EX10: Sidm 1D 38
Bramble Hill Ind. Est.
    EX14: Hon 3D 22
Bramble La. EX14: Hon 4C 22
Bramley Av. EX1: Heav 6G 13
Bramley Cl. EX6: Kenton 1B 46
Bramley Gdns. EX5: Whim 5A 8
Bramleys, The EX14: Hon 2G 23
Brand Cl. EX14: Hon 5E 23
Brand Rd. EX14: Hon 5E 23
Branscombe Cl. EX4: Exe 1E 25
Branscombe La. EX7: Daw 6A 46
Bredon Ct. EX2: Exe 1C 26
                    (off Manston Ter.)
Bredon La. EX9: Ott'n 3H 41
Brent Cl. EX5: Wood 5G 35
Brenton Rd. EX6: Kennf 6C 30
Brentor Cl. EX4: Exe 4F 11
Breton Way EX8: Exmth 6G 43
Bretteville Cl. EX5: Wood 5G 35
Brewers Ct. EX2: Exe 6B 4 (2H 25)
Brewery La. EX1: Heav 1D 26
                    (off North St.)
    EX10: Sidm 4C 38
Briar Cl. EX8: Exmth 1F 49
    EX14: Hon 6E 23
Briar Cres. EX2: Won 4D 26
Brickyard La. EX6: Star 1E 47
Brickyard Rd. EX5: Rock, Whim 3B 18
Bridespring Rd. EX4: Exe 3D 12
Bridespring Wlk. EX4: Exe 3D 12
Bridford Rd. EX2: Mar B 4A 26
Bridge Cotts. EX4: Exe 4B 12
    EX9: E Bud 6D 40
    EX9: Know 3E 45
Bridge Ct. EX4: Exe 2B 4
BRIDGE END 1E 37
Bridgefield EX11: Ott M 1E 21
                    (off Chineway Rd.)
Bridge Hill EX3: Top 3F 33
Bridgehill Gth. EX3: Top 3F 33
Bridge Rd. EX2: Cou W, Exmin 1H 31
    EX6: Exmin 1H 31
    EX8: Exmth 1C 48
    EX9: Bud S 3H 45
Bridge Vw. EX5: Rock 2E 17
Bridge Way EX4: Exe 3C 4
Brimpenny Rd. EX8: Exmth 6E 43
Brinkburn Ct. EX10: Sidm 6C 38
Brittany Rd. EX8: Exmth 3E 43
Britten Dr. EX2: Won 1F 27
BRIXINGTON 5F 43
Brixington Dr. EX8: Exmth 5F 43
Brixington La. EX8: Exmth 5F 43
                    (not continuous)
Brixington Pde. EX8: Exmth 5F 43
BROADCLYST 3E 7
Broadclyst Rd. EX5: Whim 3A 8
Broadclyst Sports Hall 5F 7
BROADCLYST STATION 1G 15
Broadfields Rd. EX2: Won 1G 27
Broadgate EX1: Exe 3C 4 (6H 11)
Broadleaf Cl. EX1: Pin 4A 14
Broadmead EX5: Wood 5F 35
    EX8: Exmth 5F 43
Broadmeadow Av. EX4: Exe 2F 25
BROAD OAK 6F 19
Broadoak Cl. EX11: W Hill 6F 19
Broadpark Rd. EX8: Exmth 6E 43
Broadparks Av. EX4: Pin 2A 14
Broadparks Cl. EX4: Pin 2A 14
Broad St. EX11: Ott M 2D 20
Broadview EX5: Broadc 4E 7
Broadwalk Ho. EX1: Exe 3E 5

Broadway EX2: Exe 3F 25
    EX5: Whim 4A 8
    EX5: Wood 6F 35
    EX10: Sidm 4B 38
Broadway, The EX8: Exmth 1G 49
Broadway Hill EX2: Exe 3E 25
Brockey Wlk. EX2: Sow 2H 27
Brodick Cl. EX4: Exe 3B 12
Bronte Ct. EX8: Exmth 2E 49
Bronte Ho. EX2: Won 3D 26
Brook Cl. EX1: Whip 4F 13
Brookdale EX11: Ott M 1E 21
Brooke Av. EX2: Won 3D 26
Brookfield Gdns. EX2: Alph 5H 25
Brookfield M. EX4: Exe 5H 11
Brookfield Rd. EX9: E Bud 5D 40
Brook Grn. Ter. EX4: Exe 5B 12
Brookhayes Cl. EX8: Exmth 1D 48
Brooklands Orchard
    EX11: Ott M 1E 21
Brooklands Rd. EX8: Exmth 6F 43
Brookland Ter. EX11: Ott M 2E 21
                    (off Brook St.)
Brookleigh Av. EX1: Heav 1F 27
Brooklyn Pk. EX8: Exmth 6E 43
Brook Mdw. EX8: Exmth 6E 43
    EX10: New P 1D 36
Brook Mdw. Ct. EX9: Bud S 4E 45
Brook Rd. EX9: Bud S 5G 45
Brookside EX8: Lymp 2A 42
    EX10: Sidm 2C 38
Brookside Cres. EX4: Whip 2F 13
Brook St. EX11: Ott M 2D 20
Brooks Warren EX5: Cranb 2B 16
Brookway EX1: Whip 5F 13
Broom Cl. EX2: Won 1E 27
Broom Pk. EX5: Cranb 2A 16
Browning Cl. EX2: Won 2E 27
Browning Ct. EX2: Exe 6A 4
Brownlands Cl. EX10: Sidm 4E 39
Brownlands Rd. EX10: Sidm 4E 39
Brownlees EX6: Exmin 4A 32
Brunel Cl. EX4: Exe 1A 4 (5G 11)
Brunel Rd. EX6: Star 1E 47
Brunswick St. EX4: Exe 1G 25
Buchanan Cl. EX14: Hon 5D 22
Buckerell Av. EX2: Exe 3C 26
Buckingham Cl. EX8: Exmth 2G 49
Buckingham Rd. EX2: Sow 3H 27
Buckland Wlk. EX6: Exmin 3H 31
Bucknill Cl. EX6: Exmin 4A 32
Buddle La. EX4: Exe 1F 25
Bude St. EX1: Exe 2E 5 (6A 12)
Budlake Rd. EX2: Matf 5A 26
Budleigh Hill EX9: E Bud 6D 40
BUDLEIGH SALTERTON 5G 45
BUDLEIGH SALTERTON HOSPITAL
    . . . . .4H 45
Buller Ct. EX2: Exe 6A 4 (2G 25)
Buller Rd. EX4: Exe 5A 4 (1G 25)
Bull Mdw. Rd. EX2: Exe 5E 5 (1A 26)
BULVERTON 3B 38
Bulverton Pk. EX10: Sidm 3B 38
Bunn Rd. EX8: Exmth 3F 43
Buntings, The EX6: Exmin 4H 31
Burch Cl. EX8: Exmth 5G 43
Burgmanns Hill EX8: Lymp 2A 42
Burlands, The EX14: Fen 1H 9
Burnet Cl. EX2: Won 3G 27
Burns Av. EX2: Won 3D 26
Burnside EX8: Exmth 6D 42
Burnthouse La. EX2: Won 3D 26
Burrator Dr. EX4: Exe 5E 11
BURROW
    EX5 . . . . .3G 7
    EX10 . . . . .1B 36
Burrow Cl. EX10: New P 1B 36

Burrow La. EX10: New P 1A 36
Burrow Rd. EX5: Broadc 3F 7
Burscombe La. EX10: Sidb, Sidf 1D 38
Buttery Cl. EX14: Hon 5E 23
Buttery Rd. EX14: Hon 5E 23
Butts Cl. EX14: Hon 6D 22
Butts Ct. EX2: Heav 1E 27
Butts Hill EX6: Kenton 1A 46
    EX11: Ott M 1E 21
Butts Rd. EX2: Heav 1E 27
    EX11: Ott M 1E 21
Byes, The EX10: Sidm 5D 38
Byes Cl. EX10: Sidf 1E 39
Byeside Rd. EX10: Sidm 1E 39
Byes La. EX10: Sidf 1F 39
Byron Rd. EX2: Won 1G 27
Byron Way EX8: Exmth 3E 43
BYSTOCK .4H 43
Bystock Cl. EX4: Exe 1B 4 (5H 11)
Bystock M. EX8: Exmth 4G 43
Bystock Nature Reserve 2H 43
Bystock Rd. EX8: Exmth 3F 43
Bystock Ter. EX4: Exe 1B 4 (5H 11)

C

Cadbury Gdns. EX9: E Bud 5D 40
Cadhay Cl. EX11: Ott M 2B 20
Cadhay La. EX11: Coom, Ott M 1B 20
California Cl. EX4: Exe 1B 12
Calm La. EX10: N'town 3E 37
Calthorpe Rd. EX4: Exe 4D 12
Cambridge St. EX4: Exe 5A 4 (1G 25)
Cambridge Ter. EX4: Exe 1F 5
                    (off Well St.)
    EX10: Sidm 5D 38
                    (off Salcombe Rd.)
Camelot Cl. EX4: Whip 3E 13
Camilla Ct. EX4: Exe 1D 4
Camperdown Ter. EX8: Exmth 3A 48
Campion Gdns. EX2: Won 3F 27
Campion Way EX14: Hon 6B 22
Canaan Way EX11: Ott M 2D 20
Canal Banks EX2: Exe 3A 26
Canberra Cl. EX4: Exe 2C 12
Candy's Path EX8: Lymp 2A 42
Canon Ho. EX1: Exe 3E 5
Canon Way EX2: Alph 6H 25
Canterbury Cl. EX14: Fen 1H 9
Canterbury Rd. EX4: Exe 5E 11
Canterbury Way EX8: Exmth 3G 43
Capel Cotts. EX8: L'ham 2H 49
Capel Ter. EX8: Exmth, L'ham 1H 49
Capper Cl. EX10: New P 1C 36
Carberry Av. EX8: Exmth 6C 42
Carders Ct. EX2: Exe 5B 4 (1H 25)
Carlile Rd. EX2: Won 1E 27
Carlton Hill EX8: Exmth 4C 48
Carlton Rd. EX2: Won 2F 27
Carlyon Cl. EX1: Heav 6E 13
Carlyon Gdns. EX1: Heav 6E 13
Carnegie Wlk. EX2: Cou W 5A 28
Caroline Av. EX8: Exmth 5H 27
Caroline Cl. EX8: Exmth 6F 43
Carousel Ct. EX2: Exe 6A 4 (2G 25)
Carpenter Cl. EX4: Exe 3B 4 (6H 11)
Carrington Pl. EX14: Hon 4F 23
Carslake Cl. EX10: Sidm 2F 39
Carter Av. EX8: Exmth 1C 48
Castle Farm EX11: W Hill 5G 19
Castle Gate EX6: Kenton 1B 46
Castle Hill Vw. EX10: Sidf 1E 39
Castle La. EX5: Wood 5G 35
    EX8: L'ham 2H 49
    EX9: Know 4C 44
Castle Mt. EX4: Exe 1C 4 (5H 11)

Castle St. EX4: Exe 2D 4 (6A 12)
Catacombs, The 3B 4
Cat & Fiddle Pk. EX5: Clyst M 3G 29
Cathedral Cl. EX1: Exe 3D 4 (6A 12)
Cathedral Yd. EX1: Exe 3C 4 (6H 11)
Catherine Sq. EX1: Exe 3D 4
Catherine St. EX1: Exe 3D 4 (6A 12)
Caulleston Cl. EX8: Exmth 5C 42
Causey Gdns. EX1: Pin 3A 14
Causey La. EX1: Pin 3A 14
Cavendish Rd. EX1: Heav 6D 12
Cecil Rd. EX2: Exe 6A 4 (2G 25)
Cedar Cl. EX8: Exmth 4F 43
EX14: Hon 4D 22
Cedars, The EX14: Hon 2G 23
Cedars Rd. EX2: Exe 6E 5 (1A 26)
Celia Cres. EX4: Whip 2E 13
Cembra Cl. EX14: Hon 4F 23
Central Av. EX2: Cou W 1D 32
EX4: Whip 2F 13
Chamberlain Rd.
EX2: Exe 6C 4 (2H 25)
Chambers Cl. EX10: Sidm 1C 38
Chancel Ct. EX4: Pin 3H 13
Chancel La. EX4: Pin 3H 13
Chancellor's Way EX4: Whip 2E 13
Chandlers La. EX10: Sidm 4D 38
Chandlers Wlk. EX2: Exe . . .6C 4 (2H 25)
Chanter Ct. EX2: Cou W 4E 27
Chantry Mdw. EX2: Alph 6H 25
Chapel Ct. EX2: Alph 5H 25
(off Church Rd.)
Chapel Hill EX3: Clyst G 2A 34
EX8: Exmth 3C 48
EX9: Bud S 4G 45
Chapel La. EX10: Col R 5A 36
EX11: Ott M 1E 21
Chapel Pl. EX3: Top 3F 33
Chapel Rd. EX2: Alph 5H 25
EX8: Lymp 2A 42
EX10: Sidm 6D 38
Chapel St. EX1: Exe 3D 4 (6A 12)
EX8: Exmth 3C 48
EX9: Bud S 5G 45
EX10: Sidm 6D 38
EX14: Hon 3E 23
Chapple Cl. EX6: Star 2F 47
Chard Av. EX5: Whim 4A 8
Chard Rd. EX1: Heav 6E 13
Chards Orchard EX6: Kennf 6C 30
Chardstock Cl. EX1: Sow 6H 13
Charinthay Gate EX4: Exe 4C 12
Charles St. EX14: Hon 3E 23
Charles St. EX8: Exmth 2C 48
Charlotte M. EX2: Exe 4E 5
(off Pavilion Pl.)
Charnley Av. EX4: Exe 1E 25
Chase, The EX14: Hon 2F 23
Chatham Cl. EX8: Exmth 6F 43
Chaucer Av. EX2: Won 3D 26
Chaucer Gro. EX4: Whip 4D 12
Chaucer Ri. EX8: Exmth 3D 42
Cheeke St. EX1: Exe 2F 5 (6B 12)
Cheese La. EX10: Sidm 5B 38
Chelmsford Rd. EX4: Exe 6D 10
Cheltenham St. EX4: Exe 5E 11
Cheney's La. EX14: Hon 1G 23
Chepstow Cl. EX2: Cou W 6F 27
Cheriswood Av. EX8: Exmth 6F 43
Cheriswood Cl. EX8: Exmth 6F 43
Cherry Cl. EX8: Exmth 4E 43
EX14: Hon 5B 22
Cherry Gdns. EX2: Won 2E 27
Cherry Tree Cl. EX4: Exe 1G 11
Cherry Tree Way EX5: Rock 2D 16
Cheshire St. EX8: Exmth 5G 43
Chester Cl. EX4: Exe 5E 11

Chester Ct. EX8: Exmth 2B 48
(off Manchester Rd.)
Chestnut Av. EX2: Won 3E 27
Chestnut Cl. EX8: Exmth 4E 43
Chestnut Ct. EX2: Alph 6H 25
Chestnut Way EX10: New P 1D 36
EX14: Hon 5C 22
Cheynegate La. EX4: Pin 1G 13
Cheyne Ri. EX4: Pin 2H 13
Chichester Cl. EX8: Exmth 2E 49
Chichester Ho. EX2: Won 1F 27
Chichester M. EX1: Exe 3E 5 (6A 12)
Chichester Way EX9: E Bud 5D 40
Chieftain Way EX2: Exe 6A 4 (2G 25)
Chineway Gdns. EX11: Ott M 1F 21
Chineway Rd. EX11: Ott M 1E 21
Chiseldon Ho. EX4: Exe 3G 11
(off Copplestone Dr.)
Chiverstone Rd. EX6: Kenton 1A 46
Chockenhole La. EX9: Ott'n 3H 41
Christow Rd. EX2: Mar B 4H 25
Chudleigh Rd. EX2: Alph, Matf 6H 25
Chudley Cl. EX8: Exmth 6F 43
Church Cl. EX5: Broadc 3E 7
Church Hill EX4: Pin 1G 13
EX9: Ott'n 4F 41
EX14: Hon 4F 23
Churchill Cl. EX6: Kenton 1A 46
Churchill Ct. EX8: Lymp 1A 42
Churchill Rd. EX2: Exe 2F 25
EX8: Exmth 5F 43
Church La. EX2: Exe 6A 4 (2G 25)
EX2: Won 1D 26
EX4: Exe 1E 5 (5A 12)
EX4: Pin 2H 13
EX5: Broadc 3E 7
EX5: Clyst M 4D 28
EX9: E Bud 5D 40
EX10: Sidm 6D 38
Church Path EX2: Exe 6A 4 (2G 25)
EX3: Top 3F 33
EX4: Exe 1A 4 (5G 11)
EX8: Lymp 2A 42
Church Path La. EX2: Heav 1E 27
Church Path Rd. EX2: Exe 3F 25
Church Path Ter. EX8: Lymp 3A 42
Church Rd. EX2: Alph 4H 25
EX2: Exe 6A 4 (2G 25)
EX5: Whim 4A 8
EX6: Cockw, Star 4D 46
EX8: Exmth 2C 48
EX8: Lymp 2A 42
EX10: Col R 6B 36
Church Side EX5: Clyst H 5F 15
Church Steps EX5: Wood 5F 35
(off Church Stile La.)
Church Stile EX6: Exmin 4B 32
Church Stile La. EX5: Wood 5F 35
Church St. EX2: Heav 1D 26
EX6: Kenton 1A 46
EX6: Star 1F 47
EX8: Exmth 3C 48
EX10: Sidf 1E 39
EX10: Sidm 6D 38
EX14: Hon 3E 23
Church Ter. EX2: Heav 1D 26
EX11: Ott M 2D 20
Chute St. EX1: Exe 1G 5 (5B 12)
City Arc. EX4: Exe 4C 4
City Bank EX1: Exe 3C 4
City Ind. Est. EX2: Exe 6D 4 (2A 26)
Clapperbrook La. EX2: Alph 5H 25
Clapper La. EX14: Com R, Hon 2E 23
Clapps La. EX11: Ott M 2D 20
Clara Pl. EX3: Top 3E 33

Claredale Rd. EX8: Exmth 3D 48
Claremont Fld. EX11: Ott M 3D 20
Claremont Gro. EX2: Exe 6F 5 (2B 26)
EX8: Exmth 2D 48
Claremont La. EX8: Exmth 2E 49
Clarence Ct. EX8: Exmth 2C 48
(off Meadow St.)
Clarence Pl. EX4: Exe 5B 12
Clarence Rd. EX4: Exe 5A 4 (1G 25)
EX8: Exmth 2C 48
EX9: Bud S 3G 45
Clarke Mead EX2: Won 2G 27
Claylands Vw. EX14: Hon 5D 22
Clay La. EX8: Lymp 3A 42
Clayton Rd. EX4: Exe 1A 4 (5G 11)
Cleve Ct. EX4: Exe 5E 11
Clevedon Cl. EX4: Exe 3B 12
Clevedon Pk. EX10: Sidm 4E 39
Cleveland Cl. EX1: Exe 1G 5 (5B 12)
Cleveland Gdns. EX1: Exe 1G 5
Cleveland Pl. EX8: Exmth 3B 48
Cleveland St. EX4: Exe 5A 4 (1G 25)
Cleve La. EX4: Exe 5E 11
Cleve Rd. EX4: Exe 6F 11
Cliff Bastin Cl. EX2: Won 2G 27
Clifford Cl. EX1: Whip 5F 13
Clifford Rd. EX4: Exe 4D 12
Cliff Path EX9: Bud S 6D 44
Cliff Rd. EX9: Bud S 5G 45
EX10: Sidm 6D 38
Cliff Ter. EX9: Bud S 5G 45
Clifton Ct. EX1: Exe 1H 5
Clifton Hill EX1: Exe 1H 5 (5C 12)
Clifton Hill Driving Range 2H 5
Clifton Hill Sports Centre & Ski Slope
. . . . .2H 5 (5C 12)
Clifton Rd. EX1: Exe 2G 5 (6B 12)
Clifton St. EX1: Exe 2G 5 (6B 12)
Clinton Av. EX4: Exe 4C 12
Clinton Cl. EX9: Bud S 3F 45
Clinton Sq. EX8: Exmth 3B 48
Clinton St. EX4: Exe 5A 4 (1G 25)
Clinton Ter. EX9: Bud S 3G 45
Clipper Quay EX2: Exe 6D 4 (2A 26)
Clipper Wharf EX8: Exmth 3A 48
(off Shelly Rd.)
Cliston Av. EX8: Exmth 5F 43
Cloister Rd. EX4: Exe 5D 12
Cloisters, The EX1: Exe 4D 4 (6A 12)
Cloisters Garth EX1: Exe 3D 4
(off Cathedral Cl.)
Clover Av. EX4: Exe 4E 11
Cludens Cl. EX2: Alph 6H 25
Clydesdale Ct. EX4: Exe 3G 11
Clydesdale Ho. EX4: Exe 3G 11
(off Clydesdale Rd.)
Clydesdale Ri. EX4: Exe 3G 11
Clydesdale Rd. EX4: Exe 3G 11
Clyst Av. EX5: Broadc 2G 15
Clyst Ct. EX5: Clyst M 3H 29
Clyst Halt Av. EX2: Sow 3A 28
Clyst Hayes Ct. EX9: Bud S 4E 45
Clyst Hayes Gdns. EX9: Bud S 4E 45
Clyst Heath EX2: Sow 3H 27
CLYST HONITON 4F 15
Clyst Honiton By-Pass
EX5: Clyst H 4G 15
Clyston Mill 3E 7
Clyst Rd. EX3: Top 2E 33
CLYST ST GEORGE 2A 34
CLYST ST MARY 3C 28
Clystside EX5: Clyst H 4F 15
Clyst Valley Rd. EX5: Clyst M 4D 28
Coastguard Hill EX9: Bud S 5H 45
Coastguard Rd. EX9: Bud S 4H 45
Coates Rd. EX2: Won 1F 27

Coaver Club 6G 5 (2B 26)
Coburg Field 6D 38
Coburg Grn. EX2: Sow 2H 27
Coburg Rd. EX10: Sidm 6C 38
Coburg Ter. EX10: Sidm 6C 38
COCKWOOD 3F 47
Codrington Ct. EX1: Exe 2G 5
Codrington St. EX1: Exe 2G 5 (6B 12)
Coffins La. EX6: Exmin 5H 31
COFTON 4D 46
Cofton Cl. EX6: Cockw 4F 47
Cofton Hill EX6: Cockw 3F 47
Cofton Rd. EX2: Mar B 5B 26
Coftons Country Holidays
    EX6: Star 4D 46
Colands Ct. EX2: Alph 6G 25
COLATON RALEIGH 6C 36
Colaton Ter. EX10: Sidm 5B 38
    (off Cotmaton Rd.)
Coleridge Cl. EX8: Exmth 3E 43
Coleridge Rd. EX2: Exe 2F 25
    EX11: Ott M 1F 21
Coles M. EX2: Exe 6A 4 (2G 25)
College, The EX2: Ide 4D 24
    EX11: Ott M 1D 20
College Av. EX2: Exe 4G 5 (1B 26)
College La. EX2: Ide 4B 24
    EX6: Long 4B 24
College Rd. EX1: Exe 4G 5 (1B 26)
Colleton Cl. EX8: Exmth 1E 49
Colleton Cres. EX2: Exe 5D 4 (1A 26)
Colleton Gro. EX2: Exe 6E 5 (2A 26)
Colleton Hill EX2: Exe 6D 4 (2A 26)
Colleton M. EX2: Exe 6E 5 (2A 26)
Colleton Row EX2: Exe 6E 5 (2A 26)
Colleton Way EX8: Exmth 1E 49
Collins Pk. EX9: E Bud 5D 40
Collins Rd. EX4: Exe 2B 12
Colliver La. EX9: Ott'n 6F 41
Colvin Cl. EX8: Exmth 2F 49
Coly Rd. EX14: Hon 5E 23
Combined Court Cen.
    Exeter 4E 5 (1A 26)
Combourg Cl. EX8: Exmth 4H 43
Comilla Cl. EX8: Exmth 4E 43
Commercial Rd. EX2: Exe 5B 4 (1H 25)
Commin's Rd. EX1: Heav 5D 12
Common Road, The
    EX8: Exmth 2G 43
Compass Quay EX2: Exe 6D 4 (2A 26)
Concorde Rd. EX8: Exmth 6G 43
Coney Ct. EX2: Exe 6C 4
Conifer M. EX2: Sow 3H 27
Connaught Cl. EX10: Sidm 5C 38
Connaught Rd. EX10: Sidm 5C 38
Conrad Av. EX4: Whip 4F 13
Constantine Ho. EX2: Exe 1C 4
Convent Flds. EX10: Sidm 5B 38
Convent Rd. EX10: Sidm 4B 38
Conway Ct. EX1: Exe 4F 5 (1B 26)
Conybeare Cl. EX4: Exe 5F 13
Cooksons Rd. EX6: Star 1E 47
Coolings, The EX2: Exe 6D 4
Coombe Cl. EX14: Hon 5E 23
Coombe Hayes EX10: Sidm 1D 38
Coombe St. EX1: Exe 4D 4 (1A 26)
Coopers Dray EX5: Whim 3A 8
Copperfield Cl. EX8: Exmth 6G 43
Copp Hill La. EX9: Bud S 3G 45
Coppledown Gdns. EX9: Bud S 3E 45
Copplestone Dr. EX4: Exe 3G 11
Copplestone La. EX10: Col R 5A 36
Copplestone Rd. EX9: Bud S 3G 45
Copse, The EX2: Cou W 1C 32
    EX8: Exmth 5G 43
    EX10: New P 1D 36
Copseclose La. EX5: Cranb 2A 16

Cordery Rd. EX2: Exe 3F 25
Corefields EX10: Sidf 1D 38
Core Hill Rd. EX10: Sidb, Stow 1B 38
    EX10: Sidm 2C 38
Coreway EX10: Sidf 1D 38
Coreway Cl. EX10: Sidf 1C 38
Coriolis Way Nth. EX1: Sow 5H 13
Coriolis Way Sth. EX1: Sow 6H 13
Corn Exchange
    Exeter 4C 4 (1H 25)
Cornflower Hill EX4: Exe 4D 10
Cornhill EX11: Ott M 1D 20
Cornmill Cres. EX2: Alph 5G 25
Cornwall St. EX4: Exe 1G 25
Coronation Rd. EX2: Won 2E 27
Coronation Ter. EX6: Star 1F 47
Coronet Cl. EX2: Sow 3H 27
Cotfield Cl. EX14: Hon 2F 23
Cotfield St. EX2: Exe 3A 26
Cotlands EX10: Sidm 6B 38
COTMATON 5B 38
Cotmaton Rd. EX10: Sidm 6B 38
Cotterell Rd. EX5: Broadc 2G 15
Cottey Cres. EX4: Whip 2E 13
Cottington Ct. EX10: Sidm 5C 38
Cottington Mead EX10: Sidm 5C 38
Cottles La. EX5: Wood 4G 35
Couches La. EX5: Wood 6G 35
Coulsdon Rd. EX10: Sidm 3D 38
Council La. EX5: Broadc 6G 7
COUNTESS WEAR 6F 27
Countess Wear Rd.
    EX2: Cou W 5E 27
Counties Cres. EX6: Star 2F 47
Country Ho. Est. EX5: Stre R 6C 8
Countryside Mus. 3E 41
Couper Mdws. EX2: Sow 3H 27
Courtenay EX14: Hon 4C 22
Courtenay Cl. EX6: Star 1E 47
Courtenay Gdns. EX2: Alph 6G 25
Courtenay Rd. EX2: Exe 3H 25
Courtenay Ter. EX6: Star 1F 47
Courtfield Cl. EX11: W Hill 4F 19
Courtlands La. EX8: Exmth 3B 42
Coventry Cl. EX14: Fen 1H 9
Coventry Rd. EX4: Exe 6F 11
Coverdale Rd. EX2: Exe 3H 25
Covetts EX5: Wood 5G 35
Cowick Ct. EX2: Exe 4G 25
Cowick Hill EX2: Exe 3E 25
Cowick La. EX2: Exe 3E 25
Cowick Rd. EX2: Exe 6A 4 (2G 25)
Cowick St. EX4: Exe 6A 4 (2F 25)
COWLEY 1F 11
Cowley Bri. Rd. EX4: Exe 1F 11
Cowper Av. EX2: Won 3C 26
Coysh Sq. EX3: Top 3E 33
Crabb La. EX2: Exe 4F 25
Craig Cotts. EX5: Clyst M 3D 28
Craig Ct. EX10: Sidm 5E 39
CRANBROOK 2A 16
Cranbrook Rd. EX2: Won 1E 27
Cranes La. EX9: E Bud 5D 40
Cranford EX10: Sidm 4D 38
Cranford Av. EX8: Exmth 3E 49
Cranford Cl. EX8: Exmth 3E 49
Cranford Hill Ho. EX8: Exmth 2F 49
Cranford Ho. EX8: Exmth 3F 49
Cranford Sports Club 3E 49
Cranford Vw. EX8: Exmth 3E 49
Cranmere Ct. EX2: Matf 6B 26
Crawford Gdns. EX2: Exe 3G 25
Creadly La. EX3: Top 2F 33
Crealy Adventure Pk. 5H 29
Crealy Meadows Caravan & Camping Pk.
    EX5: Clyst M 5H 29
Crediton Rd. EX5: Cow 1F 11

Creely Cl. EX2: Alph 6A 26
Crescent, The EX8: Exmth 1G 49
Crescent Mans. EX2: Exe 5F 5
Cricket Fld. Cl. EX9: Bud S 4G 45
Cricket Fld. La. EX9: Bud S 4G 45
Cricklepit La. EX1: Exe 5C 4
    (off Commercial Rd.)
Cricklepit St. EX1: Exe 5C 4 (1H 25)
Critchards EX5: Wood 6G 35
Criterion Pl. EX8: Exmth 3C 48
    (off Tower St.)
Crocker Ct. EX2: Exe 3H 25
Crockwells Cl. EX6: Exmin 5B 32
Crockwells Rd. EX6: Exmin 5B 32
Croft Chase EX4: Exe 2E 25
Cromwell Cl. EX1: Heav 1E 27
Cromwell Ter. EX2: Won 1H 27
    (off Sidmouth Rd.)
Crosscut Way EX14: Hon 4E 23
Crossingfields Dr. EX8: Exmth 6C 42
Cross La. EX10: Sidm 6D 38
    (off Fore St.)
Crossmead Vs. EX2: Exe 3D 24
Cross Vw. EX2: Alph 5H 25
Cross Vw. Ter. EX2: Ide 4E 25
Crowder's Hill EX8: Exmth 4D 42
Crown Way EX2: Sow 3H 27
Crudges La. EX8: Exmth 2C 48
Cuckoo Down La.
    EX14: Hon 5G 23
Culm Cl. EX2: Sow 2H 27
Culm Gro. EX2: Sow 2H 27
Culver Gdns. EX10: Sidm 5D 38
Culverland Cl. EX4: Exe 4B 12
Culverland Rd. EX4: Exe 4B 12
Culvery Cl. EX5: Wood 5G 35
Cumberland Cl. EX8: Exmth 6F 43
Cumberland Dr. EX2: Sow 2H 27
Cumberland Way
    EX1: Pin, Sow 4A 14
Cunningham Rd. EX8: Exmth 5F 43
Curie Mews EX2: Exe 2C 26
Curlew Way EX4: Exe 2A 12
Custance Ho. EX14: Hon 3E 23
    (off Queen St.)
Cutteridge La. EX4: White 1A 24
Cutters Wharf EX8: Exmth 3A 48
    (off Shelly Rd.)
Cygnet Ind. Units EX2: Sow 1A 28
Cygnet New Theatre 5D 4
Cypress Cl. EX14: Hon 6B 22
Cypress Dr. EX4: Exe 5F 11
Cyprus Gdns. EX8: Exmth 3E 49
    (not continuous)
Cyprus Rd. EX8: Exmth 3D 48

D

Dagmar Rd. EX8: Exmth 3C 48
Dairy Cl. EX6: Exmin 5B 32
Dairy Estate, The EX4: Pin 4H 13
Daisy Links EX4: Exe 4D 10
Dalditch La. EX9: Know 2B 44
Daleside Rd. EX4: Exe 3C 12
Danby La. EX8: Exmth 2C 48
Danby Ter. EX8: Exmth 2C 48
Dane's Rd. EX4: Exe 1D 4 (5H 11)
Danesway EX4: Pin 2A 14
Dark La. EX9: Bud S 4F 45
    EX10: Sidm 3B 38
Darnell Cl. EX10: Sidm 3D 38
Dartington Wlk. EX6: Exmin 3H 31
Darts Farm Shop. Village
    EX3: Clyst G 3H 33
Dart Wlk. EX2: Sow 2H 27
Darwin Ct. EX2: Exe 5E 5 (1A 26)

David Lloyd Leisure
Exeter 3A 28
Dawlish Pk. Ter. EX8: Exmth 3B 42
Dawlish Rd. EX2: Alph, Matf 6H 25
EX2: Matf 1G 31
EX6: Exmin 1G 31
Dawlish Sands Holiday Pk.
EX7: Daw W 6F 47
Dawlish Warren National Nature Reserve
. . . . .6H 47
Dawlish Warren National Nature Reserve
Visitor Cen. 6G 47
Dawlish Warren Rd.
EX6: Cockw, E'don 3F 47
EX7: Daw W, Star 3F 47
Dawn Cl. EX1: Heav 6E 13
Days-Pottles La. EX6: Exmin 4E 31
Deacon Cl. EX2: Alph 6H 25
Dean Clarke Gdns. EX2: Exe 4E 5
Deanery Pl. EX1: Exe 4D 4
Deans Mead EX10: Sidm 4C 38
Dean St. EX2: Exe 5E 5 (1A 26)
Deepdene Pk. EX2: Exe 6H 5 (2C 26)
Deepway Ct. EX6: Exmin 4A 32
Deepway Gdns. EX6: Exmin 4H 31
Deepway La. EX2: Matf 4F 31
(not continuous)
EX6: Exmin 4G 31
Deepways EX9: Bud S 3E 45
De La Rue Way EX4: Pin 3H 13
Delderfield Gdns. EX8: Exmth 3E 49
Delia Gdns. EX5: Rock 3D 16
Delius Cres. EX2: Won 1G 27
Denbeigh Ter. EX10: Sidm 4D 38
Denbury Ct. EX2: Mar B 6B 26
Dene Cl. EX8: Exmth 6F 43
Dening Ct. EX8: Exmth 1D 48
Denise Cl. EX2: Alph 6H 25
Denmark Rd. EX1: Exe 4F 5 (1B 26)
EX8: Exmth 1F 49
Dennesdene Cl. EX8: Exmth 4D 42
Dennysmead Ct. EX4: Exe 3G 11
(off Glenthorne Rd.)
Denver Cl. EX3: Top 2E 33
Denver Rd. EX3: Top 2E 33
Dettingen Path EX2: Won 3C 26
(off Barrack Rd.)
Devington Pk. EX6: Exmin 3H 31
Devon Cliffs Holiday Pk.
EX8: San B 4H 49
Devon County Showground (Westpoint)
. . . . .3F 29
Devon Rd. EX4: Exe 4D 12
Devonshire Ct. EX14: Hon 5B 22
Devonshire Pl. EX4: Exe 4B 12
Devonshire Rd. EX14: Hon 5A 22
Devonshire Way EX14: Hon 5C 22
Diamond Rd. EX2: Exe 6C 4 (2H 25)
Diane Cl. EX8: Exmth 3F 43
Dickens Dr. EX4: Exe 3D 26
Dick Pym Cl. EX2: Won 2G 27
Digby (Park & Ride) 3H 27
Digby & Sowton Station (Rail) 2A 28
Digby Dr. EX2: Sow 3H 27
Digby Ho. EX2: Sow 3H 27
Digby Rd. EX2: Sow 3G 27
Diggories La. EX14: Hon 3D 22
Dinan Way EX8: Exmth 3E 43
Dinan Way Trad. Est. EX8: Exmth . . .6H 43
Dince Hill Cl. EX5: Whim 4B 8
Dinham Cres. EX4: Exe 3A 4 (6H 11)
Dinham M. EX4: Exe 3B 4
Dinham Rd. EX4: Exe 3B 4 (6H 11)
Dix's Field EX1: Exe 2E 5 (6A 12)
Dock Rd. EX8: Exmth 3B 48
Doctors Wlk. EX2: Ide 3D 24
(not continuous)

DOG VILLAGE 5F 7
Dolforgan Ct. EX8: Exmth 3C 48
Dorchester Way EX8: Exmth 3F 43
Doriam Cl. EX4: Exe 2A 12
Dorset Av. EX4: Exe 2E 25
Dorset Pl. EX14: Hon 3E 23
(off New St.)
Dotton Cl. EX1: Sow 6H 13
Dotton La. EX10: New P 4C 36
Douglas Av. EX8: Exmth 4D 48
Douglas Ct. EX8: Exmth 3E 49
Dove Cl. EX14: Hon 5D 22
Dove La. EX10: Sidm 6D 38
Dove Way EX2: Sow 1H 27
Dowell St. EX14: Hon 3D 22
Down Cl. EX10: New P 2B 36
Doyle Centre, The
EX8: Exmth 1G 49
Drake Av. EX2: Won 1H 27
Drake's Av. EX8: Exmth 1F 49
EX10: Sidf 1E 39
Drakes Farm EX2: Ide 4E 25
Drakes Gdns. EX8: Exmth 1F 49
Drakes Rd. EX4: Exe 6A 4 (2G 25)
Draycott Cl. EX2: Won 2E 27
Dray Ct. EX8: Exmth 3C 48
(off Rolle Rd.)
Drew's Cl. EX6: Star 1E 47
Dreys Ct. EX1: Exe 6C 12
Drive, The EX9: Bic 3F 41
Drupe Farm Ct. EX10: Col R 6B 36
Dryden Cl. EX8: Exmth 3E 43
Dryden Rd. EX2: Won 2D 26
Dryfield EX6: Exmin 4B 32
Duchy Rd. EX14: Hon 5C 22
Ducks Orchard EX6: Exmin 5B 32
Duckworth Rd. EX2: Exe 2G 25
Duke of Cornwall Cl.
EX8: Exmth 6G 43
Dukes Cl. EX9: Ott'n 4G 41
Dukes Cres. EX8: Exmth 6G 43
Duke's Rd. EX9: Bud S 3F 45
Dunchideock Rd. EX2: Ide 6D 24
Dunnard EX10: Sidm 5C 38
(off All Saint's Rd.)
Dunning Ct. EX14: Hon 3D 22
Dunrich Cl. EX2: Exe 4G 5 (1B 26)
Dunsford Cl. EX8: Exmth 3F 49
Dunsford Gdns. EX4: Exe 3E 25
Dunsford Rd. EX2: Exe 3D 24
EX4: Exe 3D 24
Dunster Wlk. EX6: Exmin 3H 31
Dunvegan Cl. EX4: Exe 4G 11
Durbin Cl. EX14: Hon 4F 23
Durham Cl. EX1: Whip 5G 13
EX8: Exmth 3F 43
Durham Way EX14: Hon 5C 22
DURYARD 2H 11
Duryard Halls EX4: Exe 2G 11
Dutch Ct. EX3: Top 4F 33
Dyers Ct. EX2: Exe 5B 4 (1H 25)
Dyers Mdw. EX10: Sidf 1F 39

E

Eager Way EX6: Exmin 3H 31
Eagle Cotts. EX4: Exe 4A 4 (1G 25)
Eagle Hurst Ct. EX10: Sidm 5C 38
(off Cotmaton Rd.)
Eagles Nest EX2: Exe 2D 24
Eagle Way EX2: Sow 1B 28
Eagle Yd. EX4: Exe 4B 4
Earl Richards Rd. Nth. EX2: Exe 3C 26
Earl Richards Rd. Sth. EX2: Exe 4D 26
East Av. EX1: Heav 5C 12
EAST BUDLEIGH 5D 40

E. Budleigh Rd.
EX9: Bud S, E Bud 6D 40
(not continuous)
East Devon Crematorium
EX5: Stre R 1C 18
East Devon Golf Course 5E 45
EASTDON 5F 47
East Dr. EX8: Exmth 6C 42
Easter Hill La. EX6: Star 2D 46
Eastern Av. EX2: Cou W 1C 32
EASTERN TOWN 6D 38
Eastfield EX11: W Hill 5F 19
Eastgate EX1: Exe 2E 5 (6A 12)
East Gro. Rd. EX2: Exe 6F 5 (2B 26)
East John Wlk. EX1: Exe 2H 5 (6C 12)
East St. EX10: Sidm 6D 38
East Ter. EX1: Heav 6E 13
EX9: Bud S 4G 45
East Town La. EX6: Kenton 1A 46
East Wonford Hill EX1: Heav 1E 27
Eaton Dr. EX1: Exe 2F 5 (6B 12)
Eaton Ho. EX1: Exe 2F 5
Ebdons Ct. EX10: Sidm 6D 38
(off Church St.)
EBFORD 4A 34
Ebford La. EX3: Ebf 3A 34
Ebrington Rd. EX2: Exe 3H 25
Eden Way EX10: Col R 6C 36
Edgbaston Mead EX2: Won 2G 27
Edgerton Pk. Rd. EX4: Exe 4B 12
Edinburgh Cres. EX8: Lymp 1A 42
Edinburgh Dr. EX4: Exe 6E 11
Edmonton Cl. EX4: Exe 4E 13
Edmund St. EX2: Exe 5B 4 (1H 25)
Edwards Ct. EX2: Sow 2H 27
Edwin Rd. EX2: Exe 3H 25
Egham Av. EX2: Exe 3B 26
Egremont Rd. EX8: Exmth 1C 48
Egypt La. EX1: Exe 3D 4
Elaine Cl. EX4: Whip 2E 13
Elbury Cl. EX5: Broadc 4G 7
Eldertree Gdns. EX4: Exe 1A 4 (5G 11)
Elford EX8: Exmth 4D 48
Elgar Cl. EX2: Won 1G 27
Elim Cl. EX10: Sidm 4D 38
Elizabethan Ct. EX2: Exe 5E 5
(off Roberts Rd.)
Elizabeth Av. EX4: Exe 4C 12
Elizabeth Cl. EX5: Whim 4A 8
Elizabeth Rd. EX8: Exmth 5E 43
Ellards Cl. EX2: Exe 3C 26
Elliot Cl. EX11: Ott M 2C 20
Elliott Cl. EX4: Exe 2C 12
Elliott Way EX2: Sow 1H 27
Ellwood Rd. EX8: Exmth 5F 43
Elmbridge Gdns. EX4: Exe 4G 11
Elmbrook EX4: Exe 5H 11
Elm Cl. EX5: Broadc 4E 7
Elm Ct. EX6: Star 1F 47
Elmdon Cl. EX4: Exe 3B 12
Elmfield Cres. EX8: Exmth 5C 42
Elm Gro. EX8: Exmth 3B 48
Elm Gro. Av. EX3: Top 3F 33
Elm Gro. Gdns. EX3: Top 3F 33
Elm Gro. Rd. EX3: Top 2F 33
EX4: Exe 1B 4 (5H 11)
Elm La. EX8: L'ham 2H 49
Elm Rd. EX8: Exmth 2E 49
Elmside EX4: Exe 5C 12
EX9: Bud S 4G 45
Elmside Cl. EX4: Exe 5C 12
Elm Ter. EX14: Hon 3F 23
Elm Way EX10: Sidf 1D 38
Elsdon La. EX11: W Hill 5G 19
Elson Rd. EX4: Exe 4C 12
Elton Rd. EX4: Exe 4C 12
Elvestone EX9: Bud S 5H 45
(off Fore Street Hill)

Elvis Rd. EX8: Exmth 2F 49
Elwyn Rd. EX8: Exmth 2E 49
Ely Cl. EX4: Exe 6D 10
EX14: Fen 1H 9
Elysian Flds. EX10: Sidm 5C 38
Emmanuel Cl. EX4: Exe 4A 4 (1G 25)
Emmanuel Rd. EX4: Exe 1G 25
Emmasfield EX8: Exmth 2F 49
Emperor Way EX1: Sow 6A 14
Endfield Cl. EX1: Heav 6F 13
Endsleigh EX5: Broadc 3E 7
Endsleigh Cres. EX5: Clyst H 5D 14
England's Cl. EX10: Sidf 1F 39
Ennerdale Way EX4: Exe 6F 11
Ernsborough Ct. EX2: Exe 5F 5
Ernsborough Gdns.
    EX14: Hon 4D 22
Esplanade EX8: Exmth 3B 48
Esplanade, The EX10: Sidm 6C 38
Essex Cl. EX4: Exe 3E 25
Essington Cl. EX8: Exmth 4D 42
Essington Ct. EX8: Exmth 4D 42
Estuary Ct. EX8: Exmth 3A 48
Estuary Vw. EX9: Bud S 4H 45
Etonhurst Cl. EX2: Sow 3H 27
Eton Wlk. EX4: Exe 2D 24
Eureka Ter. *EX14: Hon* 4E 23
    (off Jerrard Cl.)
Eveleighs Ct. EX4: Exe 1E 5
Evergreen Cl. EX8: Exmth 4F 43
Evett Cl. EX8: Exmth 1G 49
Evran Dr. EX8: Exmth 4G 43
Excalibur Cl. EX4: Whip 3E 13
Exe Bri. Nth. EX2: Exe 5B 4 (1H 25)
Exebridge Retail Pk.
    EX4: Exe 6B 4 (2H 25)
Exe Bri. Sth. EX2: Exe 5B 4 (1H 25)
Exe Estuary Local Nature Reserve
    .4A 48
EXE ISLAND 4B 4 (1H 25)
Exe Reed Beds Nature Reserve . . .2D 32
Exe Sailing Club 3A 48
Exe St. EX3: Top 3F 33
    EX4: Exe 3B 4 (6H 11)
EXETER 3D 4 (6A 12)
Exeter Airport Bus. Pk.
    EX5: Clyst H 6A 16
Exeter Airport Ind. Est.
    EX5: Clyst H 6A 16
Exeter & Devon Crematorium
    EX2: Exe 4D 26
Exeter Arena Athletics Stadium 3F 13
Exeter Bus. Pk. EX1: Sow 5A 14
Exeter Castle 2D 4 (6A 12)
Exeter Cathedral
    (The Cathedral Church of St Peter)
    . . . . .3D 4 (6A 12)
Exeter Central Station (Rail)
    . . . . .1C 4 (5H 11)
Exeter Chiefs RUFC 4A 28
Exeter City FC
    St James' Park 5B 12
Exeter Cl. EX14: Fen 1H 9
EXETER COMMUNITY HOSPITAL (Whipton)
    .5G 13
Exeter Foyer EX1: Exe 5C 4
Exeter Golf Course 6G 27
Exeter Hill EX6: Kenton 1A 46
EXETER INTERNATIONAL AIRPORT
    .6A 16
EXETER NUFFIELD HEALTH HOSPITAL
    .2C 26
Exeter Phoenix 2D 4 (6A 12)
Exeter Picture House 4B 4
Exeter Rd. EX2: Cou W 1D 32
    EX3: Top 1D 32
    EX5: Stre R 1D 18

Exeter Rd. EX6: Kennf 5B 30
    EX6: Star 5C 46
    EX7: Daw 5C 46
    EX8: Exmth 4C 42
    EX10: New P 1A 36
    EX11: Ott M 2E 19
    EX14: Hon 4B 22
Exeter St David's Station (Rail)
    . . . . .1A 4 (5G 11)
EXETER SERVICE AREA 2B 28
Exeter Tennis Cen. 3H 11
Exeter Tenpin 6D 4 (2A 26)
Exeter Trade Cen. EX2: Mar B 6C 26
Exeter Underground Passages 2E 5
Exe Vale Rd. EX2: Cou W 5E 27
Exe Vw. EX6: Exmin 4A 32
Exe Vw. Cotts. EX4: Exe 4F 11
Exe View Rd. EX8: Lymp 1D 42
Exhibition Way EX4: Pin 3G 13
EXMINSTER 4B 32
Exminster Golf Course 6B 32
Exminster Hill EX6: Exmin 6A 32
EXMOUTH 3C 48
Exmouth Ct. EX8: Exmth 3D 48
Exmouth Express Miniature Railway
    .4C 48
    (off Queen's Dr.)
EXMOUTH HOSPITAL 2D 48
Exmouth Lifeboat Station 4C 48
Exmouth Mus. 2C 48
Exmouth Pavilion 4C 48
Exmouth Quay 3A 48
Exmouth Rd.
    EX3: Clyst G, Ebf, Exton 4C 28
    EX5: Clyst M 4C 28
    EX8: Exmth, Lymp 1B 42
    EX9: Bud S, Know 4D 44
    EX10: Col R, New P 6B 36
Exmouth Sports Cen. 2B 48
Exmouth Station (Rail) 2B 48
Exmouth Tennis Centre & Leisure Cen.
    .1D 48
Exonia Pk. EX2: Exe 3D 24
EXTON 6A 34
Exton La. EX3: Exton 6A 34
Exton Rd. EX2: Mar B 3A 26
Exton Station (Rail) 6A 34
EXWICK 4E 11
Exwick Ct. EX4: Exe 4F 11
Exwick Hill EX4: Exe 4F 11
Exwick La. EX4: Exe 5D 10
Exwick Rd. EX4: Exe 4F 11
Exwick Vs. EX4: Exe 5F 11
Eymore Dr. EX11: W Hill 6E 19

F

Fairfax Gdns. EX2: Alph 4H 25
Fairfield Av. EX4: Whip 4G 13
Fairfield Cl. EX8: Exmth 3D 48
Fairfield Gdns. EX14: Hon 4E 23
Fairfield Rd. EX2: Alph 6H 25
    EX8: Exmth 3D 48
Fairfield Ter. EX2: Exe 6A 4 (2G 25)
Fairhazel Dr. EX4: Exe 5F 11
Fairlawn Ct. EX10: Sidm 4D 38
Fairleigh EX10: New P 1C 36
Fairlynch Mus. 5H 45
Fairmead EX10: Sidm 1B 38
Fairmead Ct. EX1: Pin 3A 14
Fair Oak Cl. EX5: Clyst H 6B 16
Fair Oak Ct. EX5: Clyst H 6B 16
Fairpark Cl. EX2: Exe 5F 5 (1B 26)
Fairpark Rd. EX2: Exe 5E 5 (1A 26)
Fairview Av. EX5: Clyst M 4F 29
Fair Vw. Rd. EX14: Hon 4E 23

Fairview Ter. EX1: Pin 3B 14
    EX8: Exmth 2D 48
Fairway, The EX4: Exe 3C 12
Falcon Rd. EX2: Sow 2A 28
Falkland Cl. EX4: Exe 2C 12
Faraday Ho. EX1: Exe 3H 5 (6C 12)
Farleys Ct. EX3: Top 3E 33
Farm Cl. EX2: Won 2G 27
Farm Hill EX4: Exe 4D 10
Farmhouse Av. EX1: Pin 4B 14
Farm Ho. Ri. EX6: Exmin 4H 31
Farm Pk. EX5: Cranb 2A 16
Farm Way EX14: Fen 1G 9
Farthings La. EX10: New P 2B 36
Featherbed La. EX8: Exmth 5C 42
Featherstone Rd. EX8: Exmth 5C 42
Felixwell Cl. *EX4: Exe* 1F 25
    (off Okehampton Rd.)
Feltrim Av. EX2: Exe 3B 26
FENITON 1H 9
Feniton Gdns. EX14: Fen 1H 9
Feniton Station (Rail) 1G 9
Ferguson Cl. EX11: Ott M 2B 20
Ferndale Cl. EX14: Hon 6B 22
Ferndale Gdns. EX2: Exe 2G 25
Ferndale Rd. EX2: Exe 2G 25
Fernpark Cl. EX2: Exe 4C 26
Ferry Rd. EX3: Top 3E 33
Filmer Way EX2: Mar B 3H 25
Fingle Cl. EX4: Exe 4E 11
Finnimore Ind. Est.
    EX11: Ott M 2C 20
Fir Cl. EX14: Hon 4D 22
Fire Beacon La. EX10: Bowd 1H 37
Firs, The EX2: Exe 3C 24
    EX6: Kennf 5A 30
    EX8: Exmth 2F 49
First Av. EX1: Heav 6D 12
    EX2: Cou W 1C 32
Fir Tree Cl. EX8: Exmth 5H 43
Fishermans Ct. *EX8: Exmth* 3A 48
    (off Victoria Rd.)
Fisher's Sq. EX4: Exe 6A 4 (2G 25)
Fitness First
    Exeter 4A 4
Fitzroy Rd. EX1: Sow 6A 14
Flayes Almshouses
    EX4: Whip 4G 13
Fleming Av. EX10: Sidm 1E 39
Fleming Way EX2: Exe 6H 5 (2C 26)
Flexton, The *EX11: Ott M* 1D 20
    (off Silver St.)
Florida Dr. EX4: Exe 2A 12
Flowerpot La. EX4: Exe 4A 4 (1G 25)
Flower St. EX5: Wood 5G 35
Floyers-Hay Ct. EX2: Exe 6C 4
FLUXTON 6B 20
Follett Rd. EX3: Top 3E 33
Ford Farm Ct. EX6: Kenton 1A 46
Fordland Bottom Rd.
    EX6: Long 4A 24
Ford La. EX11: W Hill 6F 19
Fords Rd. EX2: Exe 6C 4 (2H 25)
Fore St. EX1: Heav 1D 26
    EX2: Ide 4E 25
    EX3: Top 3F 33
    EX4: Exe 4B 4 (1H 25)
    EX6: Kenton 1A 46
    EX8: Exmth 3C 48
    EX9: Bud S 5G 45
    EX9: Ott'n 4F 41
    EX10: Sidm 6D 38
Fore St. Hill EX9: Bud S 4H 45
Fore St. M. *EX4: Exe* 4C 4
    (off Friernhay St.)
Forge Cl. EX9: Bud S 3F 45
FORTESCUE 2F 39

Fortescue Rd. EX2: Exe 3H 25
  EX10: Sidm 2F 39
Fortfield Gdns. EX10: Sidm 6C 38
Fortfield Lawn EX10: Sidm 6C 38
Fortfield Pl. EX10: Sidm 6C 38
Fortfield Ter. EX10: Sidm 6C 38
Fort Flats EX10: Sidm 6C 38
Forton Rd. EX8: Exmth 6E 43
Foundry Yd. EX10: Sidm 5D 38
  (off Salcombe Rd.)
Fountain Ct. EX4: Exe 2B 4
Fountain Hill EX9: Bud S 5F 45
Fountain Ho. EX1: Heav 1F 5
Fouracre Cl. EX4: Whip 3E 13
Four Elms Hill EX10: Harp 1E 37
Fowey Cl. EX1: Heav 5D 12
Fowler Cl. EX6: Exmin 4A 32
Foxglove Ri. EX4: Exe 4D 10
FOXHAYES 6E 11
Foxhayes Rd. EX4: Exe 6F 11
Foxholes Hill EX8: Exmth 5E 49
Fox Rd. EX1: Whip 2F 13
Foxtor Rd. EX4: Exe 4E 11
Frances Gdns. EX1: Exe 2G 5
Francis Cl. EX4: Exe 2F 25
Francis Ct. EX2: Exe 1C 26
Franklea Cl. EX11: Ott M 2D 20
Franklin St. EX2: Exe 5E 5 (1A 26)
Franklyn Cl. EX2: Exe 3F 25
Franklyn Dr. EX2: Exe 3F 25
FRANKLYN HOSPITAL 3F 25
Fraser Rd. EX8: Exmth 5F 43
Freelands Cl. EX8: Exmth 1F 49
Frewins EX9: Bud S 3F 45
Friars Ga. EX2: Exe 5D 4 (1A 26)
FRIARS GREEN 5C 4 (1H 25)
Friars Grn. EX2: Exe 5D 4
  (off Southgate)
Friars' Wlk. EX2: Exe 5D 4 (1A 26)
Friary Ct. EX1: Exe 3D 4
Friernhay Ct. EX4: Exe 4B 4
Friernhay St. EX4: Exe 4B 4 (1H 25)
Frobisher Rd. EX8: Exmth 5E 43
Frog La. EX5: Clyst M 3C 28
Frogmore Rd. EX9: E Bud 6E 41
Frog St. EX1: Exe 5B 4 (1H 25)
  EX4: Exe 5B 4 (1H 25)
Fry's La. EX10: Sidf 1E 39
Fulford Rd. EX1: Heav 5D 12
Fulford Way EX5: Wood 5G 35
Fullers Ct. EX2: Exe 5C 4 (1H 25)
Furzebrook EX11: Ott M 1E 21
Furze Ct. EX4: Exe 3E 25
Furze Rd. EX5: Wood 5G 35

G

Gables, The EX8: Exmth 3F 49
Gabriel Ct. EX2: Exe 5C 4
Gabriels Wharf EX2: Exe 3A 26
Galahad Cl. EX4: Whip 3E 13
Gallery Cl. EX14: Hon 3D 22
Galmpton Ri. EX4: Exe 3C 12
Gandy St. EX4: Exe 2C 4 (6A 12)
Garden Cl. EX2: Won 2G 27
Garden Ct. EX9: Bud S 4G 45
Gardens, The EX10: New P 1C 36
Gareth Cres. EX4: Whip 2D 12
Garland Cl. EX4: Exe 4D 10
Garratt Cl. EX8: Exmth 4E 43
Gater La. EX1: Exe 4D 4 (1A 26)
Generals Cl. EX6: Star 2E 47
Generals La. EX6: Star 2E 47
Geneva Cl. EX2: Exe 2C 26
Geneva Ct. EX2: Exe 2C 26
  (off Geneva Cl.)

Georges Cl. EX1: Whip 6F 13
George St. EX1: Exe 4C 4 (1H 25)
  EX8: Exmth 2C 48
  EX14: Hon 3E 23
Gerald Dinnis Units
  EX2: Mar B 5B 26
Gervase Av. EX2: Exe 6B 4 (1H 25)
Gerway La. EX11: Ott M 3E 21
Gibraltar Rd. EX8: Lymp 1A 42
Gibson Cl. EX8: Exmth 6G 43
Gilbert Av. EX2: Won 2G 27
Gilbrook Cl. EX5: Wood 6F 35
Gilchrist Way EX10: Sidm 4E 39
Gipsy Hill La. EX1: Pin 4B 14
Gipsy La. EX1: Pin 4B 14
  EX8: Exmth 1C 48
Gissage Vw. EX14: Hon 3D 22
Gissons La. EX6: Exmin 4B 32
Gissons La. EX6: Kenn, Kennf 6A 30
Gittisham Cl. EX1: Sow 6H 13
Glade Wlk. EX5: Clyst M 4G 29
Gladstone Rd. EX1: Exe 3H 5 (6C 12)
Glanvill Way EX14: Hon 5C 22
Glasshouse La. EX2: Cou W 6E 27
Glastonbury Cl. EX4: Whip 2E 13
Glave Saunders Av. EX2: Won 2A 28
Glebe Cl. EX8: L'ham 2H 49
  EX8: Lymp 1A 42
  EX9: Ott'n 4G 41
Glebelands EX6: Exmin 4A 32
  EX8: Lymp 1A 42
  EX10: New P 1D 36
  EX10: Sidm 5C 38
Glen Cl. EX5: Clyst M 4G 29
Glencoe EX2: Exe 5H 5 (1C 26)
Glen Farm Cres. EX14: Hon 4F 23
Glenisla Ter. EX10: Sidm 6D 38
  (off Riverside Rd.)
Glenmore Rd. EX2: Won 1E 27
Glenorchy Ct. EX8: Exmth 2C 48
  (off Exeter Rd.)
Glen Rd. EX10: Sidm 6C 38
Glenthorne Rd. EX4: Exe 3G 11
Glenview EX14: Hon 4F 23
Glen Wlk. EX4: Exe 2B 12
Glenwood Ri. EX2: Exe 2B 26
Globefield EX3: Top 3F 33
Globe Hill EX5: Wood 5F 35
Globe La. EX3: Top 3F 33
Globe Ley EX3: Top 3F 33
  (off Globefield)
Gloucester Cl. EX14: Hon 4C 22
Gloucester Cres. EX14: Hon 5B 22
Gloucester Rd. EX4: Exe 5E 11
  EX8: Exmth 4F 43
Goat Wlk. EX3: Top 5F 33
Godfrey Cl. EX11: Ott M 2C 20
Goldsmith St. EX1: Heav 6D 12
  EX4: Exe 3C 4 (6H 11)
Gold St. EX11: Ott M 2D 20
Good Shepherd Dr.
  EX2: Exe 5E 5 (1A 26)
GOOSEMOOR 2A 36
Gordon Rd. EX1: Exe 1H 5 (5C 12)
  EX3: Top 2E 33
Gordon's Pl. EX1: Heav 1D 26
Gore La. EX8: Exmth, San B 4G 49
Gorfin Cl. EX8: Exmth 1G 49
Gorse Ho. EX4: Exe 4E 11
Gorse La. EX8: Exmth 3F 43
Gorseway EX10: Sidm 5B 38
Gosceline Wlk. EX14: Hon 5E 23
Grace Rd. Central EX2: Mar B 4A 26
Grace Rd. Sth. EX2: Mar B 5B 26
Grace Rd. W. EX2: Mar B 4H 25
Grafton Rd. EX4: Exe 3G 11
Grainger Cl. EX2: Won 1G 27

Granary La. EX9: Bud S 3H 45
Grandisson Ct. EX2: Cou W 4E 27
Grandisson Dr. EX11: Ott M 2F 21
Grange, The EX2: Exe 2C 26
Grange Av. EX8: Exmth 6D 42
Grange Cl. EX8: Exmth 1D 48
  EX8: Lymp 2B 42
Grange Cotts EX5: Rock 2F 17
Gras Lawn EX2: Exe 2C 26
Grasmere Ct. EX4: Exe 1F 25
  (off Lakelands Dr.)
Grasslands Dr. EX1: Pin 4B 14
Gratton Pk. EX5: Cranb 2B 16
Great Exmouth OO Model Railway, The
  . . . . .4D 48
Great Hill Vw. EX2: Exe 2C 12
Gt. Western Bus. Pk. EX14: Hon 5B 22
Greatwood Ter. EX3: Top 3E 33
Grecian Way EX2: Won 2G 27
Green, The EX2: Ide 5D 24
  EX5: Whim 4A 8
  EX8: L'ham 2H 49
  EX9: Ott'n 4G 41
Greenacre EX5: Rock 2E 17
Greenacres EX4: Exe 1G 11
Greenacres Cl. EX14: Fen 1H 9
Greenbank EX10: New P 1C 36
Green Cl. EX8: Exmth 1E 49
  EX9: Ott'n 4G 41
  (off Maunder's Hill)
Greendale Bus. Pk. EX5: Wood S . . .1H 35
Greendale La. EX5: Clyst M 6H 29
Greenford Vs. EX2: Exe 6C 4 (2H 25)
Greenhaven EX9: Bud S 3F 45
Greenhill Av. EX8: Exmth 2E 49
  EX8: Lymp 2A 42
Green La. EX3: Exton 6H 33
  EX4: Exe 1E 25
  EX14: Fen 2H 9
Green M. EX9: Bud S 4G 45
Green Mt. EX10: Sidm 4E 39
Greenpark Av. EX1: Pin 5H 13
Greenpark Rd. EX8: Exmth 5F 43
Green Tree La. EX5: Broadc 4F 7
Greenway EX2: Exe 3E 25
  EX5: Wood 5F 35
Greenway La. EX9: Bud S 1F 45
  EX10: Stow 2G 37
  EX14: Awli 1A 22
Greenwood Dr. EX2: Sow 1H 27
Grenadier Rd. EX1: Sow 5A 14
Grendon Almshouses EX1: Exe 3H 5
Grendon Bldgs. EX1: Exe 4C 4
Grendon Rd. EX1: Exe 3H 5 (6C 12)
Grenville Av. EX4: Whip 4H 13
Grenville Rd. EX8: Exmth 5E 43
Greyfriars Rd. EX4: Exe 4D 12
Gribble La. EX5: Rock 1F 17
Grigg's La. EX10: Sidm 2F 39
Grindle Way EX5: Clyst M 4D 28
Gronau Cl. EX14: Hon 5E 23
Grooms, The EX10: Sidm 6D 38
  (off Russell St.)
Grosvenor Mans. EX10: Sidm 6D 38
  (off Church St.)
Grosvenor Pl. EX1: Exe 1G 5 (5B 12)
Grove, The EX4: Pin 2A 14
  EX10: Sidm 5D 38
Grove Hill EX3: Top 3F 33
Grove Rd. EX5: Whim 4B 8
Guardian Rd. EX1: Sow 6A 14
Guildford Cl. EX4: Exe 5E 11
Guildhall
  Exeter 3C 4
Guildhall Shop. Cen. EX4: Exe 3C 4
Guinea St. EX1: Exe 4C 4 (1H 25)
Guinevere Way EX4: Whip 3E 13

Guinness La. EX4: Exe 4E 11
Gussiford La. EX8: Exmth 3C 48
Guys Rd. EX4: Exe 6F 11

H

Haccombe Cl. EX4: Exe 1E 25
Hacker Cl. EX10: New P 2D 36
Haddeo Dr. EX2: Sow 2H 27
Hadrian Dr. EX4: Exe 6E 11
Hadrians Way EX8: Exmth 6F 43
Haldon Cl. EX3: Top 2E 33
Haldon Ct. EX8: Exmth 5C 42
Haldon Rd. EX4: Exe 2A 4 (6G 11)
Haldon Vw. Ter. EX2: Won 1D 26
Hale La. EX14: Hon 3G 23
Haley Cl. EX8: Exmth 5E 43
Halscombe La. EX2: Ide 6A 24
Halsdon Av. EX8: Exmth 6C 42
Halsdon La. EX8: Exmth 6C 42
Halsdon Rd. EX8: Exmth 2C 48
Halsdown Gdns. EX8: Exmth 5C 42
Halse Hill EX9: Bud S 4F 45
Halses Cl. EX4: Exe 4D 10
Halse's La. EX10: N'town 6E 37
HALSFORDWOOD 4A 10
Halsfordwood La. EX4: Hals 4A 10
Halt, The EX2: Alph 5H 25
Halyards EX3: Top 3E 33
　　EX8: Exmth 3A 48
Hambeer La. EX2: Exe 3E 25
Hamilton Av. EX2: Won 4D 26
Hamilton Cl. EX10: Sidf 1F 39
Hamilton Ct. EX8: Exmth 3D 48
Hamilton Dr. EX2: Sow 1H 27
Hamilton Gro. EX6: Star 2F 47
Hamilton La. EX8: Exmth 2D 48
Hamilton Rd. EX3: Top 2E 33
　　EX8: Exmth 2F 49
Ham La. EX10: Sidm 6D 38
HAMLET 5B 22
Hamlin Gdns. EX1: Heav 5E 13
Hamlin La. EX1: Heav 5E 13
Hamlyns La. EX4: Exe 3D 10
Hammond Cft. Way EX2: Alph 6H 25
Hampden Pl. EX2: Exe 6B 4
Hampshire Cl. EX4: Exe 2E 25
Hampton Bldgs. EX4: Exe 5B 12
Hams, The EX2: Ide 5D 24
HAND AND PEN 1B 18
Hand and Pen Cotts. EX5: Whim 1B 18
Handsford Way EX11: Ott M 2C 20
Hanover Cl. EX1: Heav 6D 12
Hanover Ct. EX2: Matf 6A 26
Hanover Rd. EX1: Heav 6D 12
Hansford Ct. EX14: Hon 4E 23
Harbour Ct. EX8: Exmth 3B 48
Harbour Way EX6: Cockw 3F 47
　　　　　　(off Cofton Hill)
Harcombe Flds. EX10: Sidf 1F 39
Harcombe La. EX10: Sidf 1F 39
Harcombe La. E. EX10: Sidf 1G 39
Hardy Rd. EX2: Won 1H 27
Hardy's Ct. EX10: Col R 5B 36
Harebell Copse EX4: Exe 4D 10
HAREFIELD 1C 42
Harefield Cl. EX4: Exe 4G 11
Harefield Cotts. EX8: Lymp 2A 42
Harefield Dr. EX8: Lymp 2B 42
Harefield Rd. EX8: Lymp 1B 42
Harlequins Shop. Cen. EX4: Exe 2C 4
HARPFORD 1E 37
Harrier Ct. EX5: Clyst H 6C 16
Harrier Way EX2: Sow 2A 28
Harringcourt Rd. EX4: Pin 2A 14
Harrington Dr. EX4: Pin 2A 14

Harrington Gdns. EX4: Pin 3A 14
Harrington La. EX4: Pin 2G 13
Hartley Rd. EX8: Exmth 3C 48
Hartopp Rd. EX8: Exmth 1C 48
Harts Cl. EX1: Pin 4A 14
Harts La. EX1: Pin, Whip 4G 13
　　　　　　(not continuous)
Harwood Cl. EX8: Exmth 6F 43
Hatcher Cl. EX14: Hon 6E 23
Hatchland Rd. EX4: Polt 4B 6
Hatherleigh Rd. EX2: Exe 4G 25
HAVEN BANKS 2A 26
Haven Banks EX2: Exe 6C 4 (2H 25)
Haven Banks Outdoor Education Cen.
　　　　　　..................6D 4 (2A 26)
Haven Banks Retail Pk.
　　EX2: Exe 6C 4 (2H 25)
Haven Cl. EX2: Exe 2H 25
Haven Rd. EX2: Exe 6B 4 (2H 25)
Hawkerland Rd. EX10: Col R 5A 36
Hawkins La. EX11: W Hill 6F 19
Hawthorn Cl. EX14: Hon 4D 22
Hawthorn Dr. EX10: Sidm 1B 38
Hawthorn Gro. EX8: Exmth 6G 43
Hawthorn Rd. EX2: Won 3D 26
Hawthorn Way EX2: Alph 6G 25
Haydons Pk. EX14: Hon 4E 23
Hayes Barton Ct. EX4: Exe 4A 4 (1G 25)
Hayes Cl. EX9: Bud S 3G 45
　　EX9: Ott'n 4G 41
Hayes La. EX9: E Bud 4A 40
Hayes Sq. EX5: Cranb 2A 16
Hayeswood La. EX9: E Bud 6A 40
Haymans Orchard EX5: Wood 5G 35
Hayne Cl. EX4: Exe 5E 13
Hayne La. EX14: Gitt 5A 22
Haynes La. EX6: Long 4A 24
Haytor Dr. EX4: Exe 5E 11
Hazel Cl. EX10: New P 1D 36
Hazeldene Gdns. EX8: Exmth 6C 42
Hazel Gro. EX5: Rock 3E 17
Hazelmead Rd. EX5: Clyst M 4F 29
Hazel Rd. EX2: Won 4D 26
Hazelwood Cl. EX14: Hon 5E 23
Headingley Cl. EX2: Won 2G 27
Headland Cl. EX1: Whip 5G 13
Headland Cres. EX1: Whip 5G 13
Headon Gdns. EX2: Cou W 5E 27
Heard Av. EX8: Exmth 1G 49
Hearts of Oak EX2: Sow 1A 28
Heath Cl. EX14: Hon 5B 22
Heather Cl. EX1: Whip 6F 13
　　EX14: Hon 6B 22
Heatherdale EX8: Exmth 3E 49
Heather Grange EX11: W Hill 6F 19
Heathers, The EX8: Exmth 2F 49
Heathpark Ind. Est. EX14: Hon 5B 22
Heathpark Way EX14: Hon 4B 22
Heath Rd. EX2: Won 2F 27
HEAVITREE 6E 13
Heavitree Pk. EX1: Heav 1E 27
Heavitree Rd. EX1: Exe 2F 5 (6B 12)
Hele Rd. EX4: Exe 1A 4 (5G 11)
Hellier Cl. EX14: Hon 5C 22
Hellings Gdns. EX5: Broadc 3E 7
Hellings Pk. La. EX5: Broadc 6G 7
Heneaton Sq. EX2: Cou W 6F 27
Henley Rd. EX8: Exmth 2E 49
Hennis, The EX4: Exe 1E 5
Hennock Ct. EX2: Mar B 5B 26
Hennock Rd. Central EX2: Mar B ...5A 26
Hennock Rd. E. EX2: Mar B 5B 26
Hennock Rd. Nth. EX2: Mar B 4A 26
Henrietta Pl. EX4: Exe 2B 4
　　EX8: Exmth 2C 48
　　　　　　(off Clarence Rd.)

Henrietta Rd. EX8: Exmth 2C 48
Henry Lewis Cl. EX5: Whim 4A 8
Henrys Run EX5: Cranb 2A 16
Hensford M. EX7: Daw 6A 46
Hensford Rd. EX7: Daw 6A 46
Hensleigh Dr. EX2: Exe 4H 5 (1C 26)
Heraldry Row EX2: Sow 2H 27
　　　　　　(off Heraldry Way)
Heraldry Wlk. EX2: Sow 2H 27
　　　　　　(off Heraldry Way)
Heraldry Way EX2: Sow 2H 27
Herbert Rd. EX1: Heav 5D 12
Hereford Cl. EX8: Exmth 3F 43
Hereford Rd. EX4: Exe 6D 10
Heritage Ct. EX14: Hon 3E 23
Heritage Grange EX8: Exmth 2E 49
Heritage Way EX10: Sidm 1D 38
Heron Ct. EX8: Exmth 3E 49
Heron Rd. EX2: Exe 3D 24
　　EX2: Sow 1A 28
　　EX14: Hon 5D 22
Herschell Rd. EX4: Exe 4C 12
Hexworthy Av. EX4: Exe 5C 11
Heydon's La. EX10: Sidm 5C 38
Heywood Dr. EX6: Star 1E 47
Hickory Cl. EX14: Hon 4G 23
Hides Rd. EX10: Sidm 1E 39
High Bank EX11: W Hill 6F 19
Highbury Pk. EX8: Exmth 6C 42
Highcliffe Cl. EX8: Lymp 3A 42
Highcliffe Ct. EX8: Lymp 3A 42
High Cft. EX4: Exe 3G 11
Highcroft Ct. EX4: Exe 3G 11
Highcross Rd. EX4: Exe 4A 12
Higher Aboveway EX6: Exmin 5B 32
Higher Barley Mt. EX4: Exe 6E 11
Higher Bedlands EX9: Bud S 3F 45
Higher Brand La. EX14: Hon 6E 23
Higher Broad Oak Rd.
　　EX11: High M, W Hill 6F 19
Higher Brook Mdw. EX10: Sidf 1E 39
Higher Down EX6: Kenton 1A 46
Higher Duryard EX4: Exe 1A 12
Higher Exwick Hill EX4: Exe 5E 11
Higher Fortescue EX10: Sidm 2F 39
Higher Greenway La.
　　EX10: Sidm, Stow 1H 37
Higher Hill Vw. EX14: Hon 4C 38
Higher Hoopern La. EX4: Exe 3A 12
　　　　　　(not continuous)
Higher King's Av. EX4: Exe 3B 12
Higher Marley Rd. EX8: Exmth 3F 43
Higher Marshrow EX6: Exmin 6C 32
Higher Maunders Hill EX9: Ott'n ...5G 41
Higher Mdw. EX5: Cranb 3A 16
Higher Ridgeway EX11: Ott M 1E 21
Higher Rd. EX5: Wood S 1E 35
Higher Shapter Cl. EX3: Top 4F 33
Higher Shapter St. EX3: Top 4F 33
Higher Spring Gdns.
　　EX11: Ott M 2E 21
Higher Summerlands
　　EX1: Exe 2G 5 (6B 12)
Higher Way EX10: Harp 1E 37
HIGHER WEAR 5D 26
Higher Wear Rd. EX2: Cou W 1C 32
HIGHER WOOLBROOK 2B 38
Higher Woolbrook Pk.
　　EX10: Sidm 2B 38
Highfield EX3: Top 1F 33
　　EX10: Sidm 4C 38
　　　　　　(off Brewery La.)
Highfield La. EX8: Exmth 3D 48
Highlands EX11: Ott M 2D 20
High Mdw. EX10: Sidm 2D 38
High Mdws. EX4: Exe 1E 25

High St. EX2: Ide 5D 24
  EX3: Top 2E 33
  EX4: Exe 3C 4 (6H 11)
  EX6: Kenton 1A 46
  EX8: Exmth 3C 48
  EX9: Bud S 5G 45
  EX9: E Bud 5D 40
  EX10: New P 1B 36
  EX10: Sidm 5D 38
  EX14: Hon 4D 22
High Vw. EX14: Fen 1H 9
High Vw. Gdns. EX8: Exmth 2D 48
Hill Barton Bus. Pk.
  EX5: Clyst M 3H 29
Hill Barton Cl. EX1: Whip 5G 13
Hill Barton La. EX1: Whip 5G 13
  (not continuous)
Hill Barton Rd. EX1: Sow, Whip 4H 13
  EX2: Sow 1H 27
Hillborough EX5: Wood 5G 35
Hill Cl. EX4: Exe 3B 12
Hill Cres. EX14: Hon 3F 23
Hill Crest EX6: Exmin 4A 32
Hillcrest EX11: Ott M 2D 20
Hillcrest Pk. EX4: Exe 2A 12
Hill Dr. EX8: Exmth 4D 42
Hill La. EX1: Whip 4F 13
  (not continuous)
Hill Pond Caravan & Camping Site
  EX5: Clyst M 4H 29
Hill Ri. EX1: Whip 5G 13
Hillsborough Av. EX4: Exe 5A 12
Hillside EX10: New P 1B 36
  EX11: W Hill 4G 19
Hillside Av. EX4: Exe 5A 12
Hillside Rd. EX10: Sidm 5D 38
Hill Vw. EX10: Sidm 4D 38
  EX11: Ott M 2D 20
Hillway La. EX10: N'town 2E 37
Hillyfield Rd. EX1: Whip 5G 13
Hind St. EX11: Ott M 1E 21
HMP Exeter EX4: Exe 1C 4 (5H 11)
Hoker Rd. EX2: Won 1E 27
Holland Hall EX4: Exe 3G 11
Holland Rd. EX2: Exe 2F 25
  EX8: Exmth 6F 43
Holley Cl. EX6: Exmin 4A 32
Hollis Cl. EX11: Ott M 1E 21
Holloway St. EX2: Exe 5D 4 (1A 26)
Hollow La. EX1: Pin 5H 13
Hollowpits Ct. EX2: Alph 6H 25
Hollows, The EX8: Exmth 2D 48
Holly Ball La. EX5: Whim 3C 8
Holly Cl. EX5: Broadc 3E 7
  EX14: Hon 5E 23
Hollymount Cl. EX8: Exmth 4E 43
Holly Rd. EX2: Won 3D 26
Holly Wlk. EX8: Exmth 4F 43
Holman Way EX3: Top 4F 33
Holmdale EX10: Sidm 5D 38
Holne Ct. EX4: Exe 4E 11
Holne Ri. EX2: Won 1F 27
Holt, The EX14: Hon 2G 23
Holyshute Gdns. EX14: Hon 2F 23
  (off Monkton Rd.)
Homeclyst Ho. EX2: Exe 6B 4
Homecourt Ho. EX4: Exe 4B 4
Homefield Cl. EX11: Ott M 2E 21
Homefield Rd. EX1: Heav 6D 12
Homelace Ho. EX14: Hon 4E 23
Hometor Ct. EX8: Exmth 1C 48
Honeylands Dr. EX4: Exe 5E 13
Honeylands Way EX4: Exe 5E 13
Honey La. EX1: Pin 2B 14
  EX5: Wood S 1G 35
Honey Pk. Rd. EX9: Bud S 3H 45
Honeysuckle Cl. EX4: Exe 4D 10

Honeysuckle Dr. EX14: Hon 5B 22
Honeywill Ct. EX2: Heav 1E 27
HONITON 3E 23
Honiton Bottom Rd.
  EX14: Hon 5E 23
Honiton Bus. Pk. EX14: Hon 3D 22
Honiton Caravan and Camping Club
  EX14: Hon 2G 23
Honiton Golf Course 6G 23
HONITON HOSPITAL 4E 23
Honiton Leisure Cen. 3E 23
Honiton Rd. EX1: Heav, Sow 1F 27
  EX5: Clyst H 5C 14
Honiton Road (Park & Ride) 6A 14
Honiton Station (Rail) 4E 23
Honiton Swimming Pool 2E 23
Hooker Cl. EX9: Bud S 3F 45
Hoopern Av. EX4: Exe 3A 12
Hoopern La. EX4: Exe 4A 12
Hoopern M. EX4: Exe 4H 11
Hoopern St. EX4: Exe 1D 4 (5A 12)
Hoopers Ct. EX5: Rock 2D 16
Hope Ct. EX4: Exe 4A 12
  (off Prince of Wales Rd.)
Hope Hall EX4: Exe 4A 12
Hope Pl. EX2: Won 1E 27
Hope Rd. EX2: Won 1E 27
Hornbeam Cl. EX14: Hon 5C 22
Horseguards EX4: Exe 5A 12
HOSPISCARE 2D 26
Hospital La. EX1: Whip 4G 13
Houghton La. EX10: N'town 4E 37
Houndbeare La.
  EX5: Ayle, Mar G 6A 18
Howard Cl. EX14: Hon 4E 11
Howarth Cl. EX10: Sidm 1C 38
Howell Rd. EX4: Exe 1B 4 (5G 11)
HULHAM 4D 42
Hulham Rd. EX8: Exmth 6D 42
Hulham Va. EX8: Exmth 5E 43
Hummingbird Cl. EX1: Pin 3A 14
Humphries Pk. EX8: Exmth 6F 43
Hungry Fox Est. EX5: Broadc 1G 15
Hunton Cl. EX8: Lymp 2A 42
Hurst Av. EX2: Won 2F 27
Hurst's Almshouses EX2: Exe 4E 5
Hutchings Mead EX1: Pin 4B 14
Hylands Cl. EX11: W Hill 6F 19
Hylton Gdns. EX4: Exe 6F 11

I

Ice Ho. La. EX10: Sidm 3B 38
Iddesleigh Rd. EX4: Exe 4C 12
Iddesleigh Ter. EX3: Exton 6A 34
IDE 5D 24
Ide La. EX2: Exe, Ide, Alph 3D 24
  (not continuous)
Idestone La. EX2: Ide 6C 24
Ilex Cl. EX2: Shil G 4A 30
  EX4: Whip 2F 13
Imperial Rd. EX8: Exmth 2B 48
Imperial Road Athletics Track 2B 48
Imperial St. EX4: Exe 1F 25
Inchcoulter Apartments
  EX8: Exmth 4E 49
Ingleside Ct. EX9: Bud S 4G 45
Inglewood Ho. EX4: Exe 5B 12
  (off Sidwell St.)
Inner Ting Tong EX9: Know 2C 44
Iolanthe Dr. EX4: Whip 2E 13
Iona Av. EX8: Exmth 5C 42
Iris Av. EX2: Exe 6B 4 (2H 25)
Iron Bri. EX4: Exe 2B 4 (6H 11)
Isaac Cl. EX9: Ott'n 4G 41
Isabel Ct. EX4: Exe 6A 4 (2G 25)

Isambard Pde. EX4: Exe 5G 11
Isca Bowls & Bridge Cen. 3G 13
Isca Lofts EX4: Exe 1E 5
Isca Rd. EX2: Exe 6C 4 (2H 25)
  EX8: Exmth 4E 49
Isis Cl. EX14: Hon 2G 23
Isleworth Rd. EX4: Exe 1E 25
Iveagh Ct. EX4: Exe 4F 11
Ivy Cl. EX2: Won 2E 27
  EX10: Sidm 2D 38
Ivydale EX8: Exmth 4F 43

J

Jacketts EX9: Ott'n 4G 41
JACK-IN-THE-GREEN 2C 16
Jack Sadler Way EX2: Cou W 5A 28
Jackson Mdw. EX8: Lymp 2A 42
James Cl. EX1: Exe 4D 4 (1A 26)
James Owen Ct. EX4: Exe 1F 5
Jarvis Bungs. EX8: Exmth 2G 49
Jarvis Cl. EX8: Exmth 2G 49
Jefford Ho. EX4: Exe 3G 11
Jennifer Cl. EX2: Exe 3C 26
Jerrard Cl. EX14: Hon 4E 23
Jerrard Cres. EX14: Hon 4E 23
Jesmond Rd. EX1: Exe 1H 5 (5C 12)
Jesu St. EX11: Ott M 2D 20
Jocelyn Rd. EX9: Bud S 3G 45
John Hannam Ho. EX1: Exe 2F 5
John Hudson Way
  EX8: Exmth 2G 49
John Levers Way EX4: Exe 6F 11
John St. EX1: Exe 4C 4 (1H 25)
Joslin Cl. EX14: Hon 5C 22
Jubilee Cl. EX6: Exmin 4B 32
Jubilee Ct. EX4: Exe 2B 4
Jubilee Dr. EX8: Exmth 4E 43
Jubilee Gdns. EX10: Sidm 1E 39
Jubilee Gro. EX8: Lymp 2B 42
Jubilee Rd. EX1: Heav 5C 12
Jubilee Sq. EX3: Top 4F 33
Julius Ho. EX4: Exe 1C 4
Juniper Cl. EX4: Whip 2F 13
  EX14: Hon 5C 22
Jupes Cl. EX6: Exmin 5B 32
Jutland Way EX2: Cou W 5H 27

K

Kalendarhay La. EX1: Exe 3C 4 (6H 11)
Katherines La. EX11: Ott M 1E 21
Kay Cl. EX8: Exmth 1E 49
Keats Cl. EX8: Exmth 3E 43
Keegan Cl. EX11: Ott M 2B 20
Keepers Cotts. EX9: Know 4C 44
Kemps Fld. EX5: Cranb 2A 16
Kenandy Cl. EX10: Sidm 6C 38
Kenbury Cres. EX6: Cockw 3F 47
Kenbury Dr. EX2: Alph 6A 29
Kendall Cl. EX4: Exe 1G 5 (5B 12)
KENN 6B 30
Kennaway Rd. EX11: Ott M 1E 21
Kennerley Av. EX4: Whip 4F 13
KENNFORD 5B 30
Kennford Intl. Caravan Pk.
  EX6: Kennf 6A 30
Kennford Rd. EX2: Mar B 3H 25
Kenn La. EX6: Exmin 6H 31
Kent Cl. EX2: Won 2E 27
KENTON 1A 46
Kenton Hill EX6: Kenton 1B 46
Kenton M. EX6: Kenton 1A 46
  (off Fore St.)
Kenton Pl. EX2: Mar B 4A 26

KERSBROOK 3G 45
Kersbrook La. EX9: Bud S 2G 45
Kerslake's Ct. EX14: Hon 3E 23
Kerswill Rd. EX4: Exe 2F 25
Kestell Rd. EX10: Sidm 5E 39
Kestor Dr. EX4: Exe 4E 11
Kestrel Bus. Pk. EX2: Sow 1B 28
Kestrel Way EX2: Sow 1A 28
Keverel Rd. EX8: Exmth 6C 42
Kilbarran Ri. EX4: Exe 4G 11
Killerton Wlk. EX6: Exmin 3H 31
                        (off Devington Pk.)
Kilmorie Hall EX4: Exe 4A 12
Kimberley Rd.
   EX2: Exe 5E 5 (1A 26)
King Alfred Way EX10: New P 1C 36
King Arthur's Rd. EX4: Whip 2D 12
King Charles Way EX10: Sidm 1D 38
Kingdom M. EX4: Exe 5G 11
King Edward St. EX4: Exe 3G 11
King Edward Studios EX4: Exe 3G 11
Kingfisher Av. EX2: Exe 2D 24
Kingfisher Ct. EX4: Pin 3H 13
Kingfisher Dr. EX4: Exe 2B 12
Kingfisher Way EX2: Sow 1A 28
King Henrys Rd. EX2: Exe 3C 26
Kings Av. EX11: Ott M 1F 21
Kings Ct. EX14: Hon 3E 23
                              (off New St.)
Kings Dwellings EX1: Exe 4C 4
                            (off King St.)
Kings Gdns. EX14: Hon 3E 23
                       (off Kerslakes Ct.)
Kingsgate EX4: Exe 4A 12
Kingsgate Bus. Cen. EX14: Hon 5C 22
Kingslake Ct. EX8: Exmth 1C 48
Kingslake Ri. EX8: Exmth 1C 48
Kings La. EX10: Sidm 6D 38
Kingsley Av. EX4: Whip 4F 13
Kings M. EX14: Hon 4D 22
Kings Pk. EX14: Hon 3E 23
                            (off King St.)
King's Rd. EX4: Exe 4C 12
   EX14: Hon 3F 23
King Stephen Cl. EX4: Exe 5A 12
King's Ter. EX14: Hon 3E 23
Kingston Rd. EX8: Exmth 2E 49
King St. EX1: Exe 4C 4 (1H 25)
   EX8: Exmth 3C 48
   EX14: Hon 4D 22
King St. Business Pk. EX1: Exe 4C 4
Kingsway EX2: Heav 1D 26
King's Wharf EX2: Exe 5D 4
Kingswood Cl. EX4: Exe 4E 11
King William St.
   EX4: Exe 1E 5 (6A 12)
Kinnerton Ct. EX4: Exe 4F 11
Kinnerton Way EX4: Exe 4D 10
Kipling Cl. EX8: Exmth 4E 43
Kipling Dr. EX2: Won 2D 26
Kitts La. EX10: N'town 2E 37
Knapp Hill EX10: Sidm 4C 38
Knighthayes Wlk. EX6: Exmin 4H 31
Knightly Rd. EX2: Exe 3C 26
Knights Cres. EX2: Sow 3H 27
Knights Pl. EX4: Whip 3D 12
Knightstone EX11: Ott M 4F 21
Knightstone La. EX11: Ott M 4F 21
Knightstone Rd. EX11: Ott M 4E 21
KNOWLE 3E 45
Knowle Bus. Units EX2: Mar B 5B 26
Knowle Ct. EX14: Hon 3E 23
Knowle Dr. EX4: Exe 6E 11
   EX10: Sidm 5B 38
Knowle Gdns. EX10: Sidm 5B 38
Knowle Hill EX9: Know 3C 44
Knowle M. EX9: Know 2D 44

Knowle Rd. EX9: Bud S, Know 3E 45
Knowle Village EX9: Know 4D 44

L

Laburnum Cl. EX8: Exmth 4F 43
   EX14: Hon 5B 22
Laburnum Rd. EX2: Won 3D 26
Lace Wlk. EX14: Hon 3E 23
Lackaborough Ct. EX2: Alph 6G 25
Ladram Rd. EX9: Ott'n 4H 41
Ladymead EX10: Sidm 1B 38
Ladysmith La. EX1: Heav 6D 12
Ladysmith Rd. EX1: Heav 5D 12
Lafrowda EX4: Exe 4A 12
Lake Cl. EX14: Hon 4F 23
Lakelands Dr. EX4: Exe 6F 11
Lakeside Av. EX2: Cou W 6F 27
Lamacraft Dr. EX4: Exe 5E 13
Lamb All. EX1: Exe 3D 4
Lamplough Rd. EX8: Exmth 4C 42
Lancaster Cl. EX2: Won 1F 27
Lancaster Ct. EX5: Clyst H 6A 16
Lancelot Rd. EX4: Whip 2E 13
Landhayes Rd. EX4: Exe 1F 25
LAND PART .4C 38
Landscore Rd. EX4: Exe 1F 25
Lands Rd. EX4: Pin 3H 13
Langaton Gdns. EX1: Pin 3B 14
Langaton La. EX1: Pin 3B 14
Langdon Bus. Pk. EX5: Clyst M 4F 29
LANGDON HOSPITAL 6C 46
Langerwehe Way EX8: Exmth 3B 48
Langford Av. EX14: Hon 3F 23
Langford Rd. EX14: Hon 2F 23
                          (not continuous)
Langstone Dr. EX8: Exmth 5E 43
Lansdowne EX2: Won 2F 27
Lansdowne Rd. EX9: Know 4D 44
Lansdowne Ter. EX2: Exe . . .5E 5 (1A 26)
Lansport La. EX7: Daw 6B 46
Larch Cl. EX8: Exmth 4F 43
Larch Rd. EX2: Exe 3F 25
LARKBEARE
   EX2 . . . . .6E 5 (2A 26)
   EX5 . . . . .3G 9
Larkbeare Av. EX5: Lark 4G 9
Larkbeare Rd. EX2: Exe 6E 5 (2A 26)
Lark Cl. EX4: Exe 3B 12
Lark Ri. EX10: New P 1C 36
Laskeys La. EX10: Sidm 5E 39
Latimer Rd. EX4: Whip 4E 13
Laurel Ri. EX8: Exmth 1F 49
Laurel Rd. EX2: Won 3D 26
   EX14: Hon 5B 22
Laurels, The EX10: Sidm 4C 38
Lavender Rd. EX2: Exe 4E 11
Lawn, The EX9: Bud S 5G 45
Lawn Rd. EX8: Exmth 2C 48
Lawn Vista EX10: Sidm 4D 38
Lawrence Av. EX4: Exe 2G 25
Lawrence Wlk. EX6: Exmin 3H 31
Laxton Av. EX1: Heav 6G 13
Lazenby EX4: Exe 4A 12
Lea La. EX9: Ott'n 4G 41
                          (not continuous)
Lea Rd. EX9: Ott'n 4G 41
Leas Rd. EX9: Bud S 4G 45
Leatside EX1: Exe 5C 4
                        (off Commercial Rd.)
Lebanon Cl. EX4: Exe 3C 12
Lee Cl. EX14: Hon 3D 22
Leeward Ct. EX8: Exmth 3A 48
Legion Way EX2: Alph 5H 25
Leicester Mead EX4: Exe 5E 11
Leigham Bus. Units EX2: Mar B 6B 26

Leighdene Cl. EX2: Exe 6H 5 (2C 26)
Leighton Ter. EX4: Exe 1E 5 (5A 12)
Le Locle Cl. EX10: Sidm 1B 38
Lennox Av. EX10: Sidm 5D 38
Leslie Rd. EX8: Exmth 1C 48
Lestock Cl. EX8: L'ham 2G 49
Lethbridge Rd. EX2: Won 1F 27
Lewis Cres. EX2: Sow 3H 27
Leypark Cl. EX1: Whip 5G 13
Leypark Cres. EX1: Whip 6G 13
Leypark Rd. EX1: Whip 5G 13
Liberty Way EX2: Cou W 5H 27
Lichfield Rd. EX4: Exe 6D 10
Lichgate Rd. EX2: Alph 6H 25
Liffey Ri. EX4: Exe 4E 11
Lilac Rd. EX2: Won 3D 26
Lillage La. EX9: E Bud 5C 40
Lilley Wlk. EX14: Hon 4F 23
Lily Mt. EX4: Exe 4D 10
Lilypond La. EX5: Whim 4C 8
Lime Cl. EX5: Broadc 4E 7
Lime Gro. EX6: Exmin 3A 32
   EX8: Exmth 4E 43
Limegrove Rd. EX4: Exe 1F 25
Lime Kiln La. EX2: Cou W 5E 27
Limekiln La. EX8: Exmth 4E 49
Lime Tree Cl. EX2: Won 3G 27
Lincoln Cl. EX8: Exmth 3G 43
   EX14: Fen 1H 9
Lincoln Rd. EX4: Exe 6E 11
Linda Cl. EX1: Heav 1F 27
Lindemann Cl. EX10: Sidm 1C 38
Linden Cl. EX8: Exmth 5F 43
Linden Va. EX4: Exe 1B 4 (5H 11)
Linfield Gdns. EX4: Exe 5E 11
Linhay Cl. EX14: Hon 6D 22
Links Cl. EX8: Exmth 2E 49
Links Rd. EX9: Bud S 5E 45
Linnet Cl. EX4: Exe 2B 12
Lisa Cl. EX2: Won 2E 27
Lister Cl. EX2: Exe 2C 26
Little Barley EX4: Exe 1F 25
Lit. Bicton Ct. EX8: Exmth 3C 48
                        (off Lit. Bicton Pl.)
Lit. Bicton Pl. EX8: Exmth 3C 48
Little Bri. Business Pk.
   EX5: Clyst M 5F 29
Lit. Castle St. EX4: Exe 2D 4 (6A 12)
Lit. Chockenhole La. EX9: Ott'n 3H 41
Little Cl. EX11: Ott M 2D 20
Littledown Cl. EX8: L'ham 2H 49
Lit. Down La. EX9: E Bud 6C 40
Littledown La. EX10: New P 3A 36
Lit. Down Orchard EX10: New P 2B 36
LITTLEHAM .2H 49
Littleham Chu. Path EX8: L'ham 5B 44
   EX9: Bud S 5D 44
Littleham Rd. EX8: Exmth, L'ham 2F 49
Littleham Village EX8: L'ham 2H 49
Lit. John's Cross Hill EX2: Exe 3E 25
LITTLE KNOWLE 4F 45
Little Knowle EX9: Bud S 4F 45
Lit. Knowle Ct. EX9: Bud S 4F 45
Littlemead La. EX8: Exmth 4C 42
Little Mdw. EX8: Exmth 4F 43
Lit. Queen St. EX4: Exe 3D 4 (6A 12)
Lit. Rack St. EX1: Exe 4C 4 (1H 25)
Little Silver EX4: Exe 2B 4 (5H 11)
Lit. Silver La. EX2: Matf 3F 31
LITTLETOWN 5D 22
Littletown Rd. EX14: Hon 5D 22
Littletown Vs. EX14: Hon 5E 23
                        (off Manor Cres.)
Littleway EX2: Exe 3F 25
Livermore Rd. EX14: Hon 4E 23
Liverpool Hill EX4: Exe 5E 11
Liverton Bus. Pk. EX8: Exmth 6H 43

Liverton Cl. EX8: Exmth 1G 49
Liverton Copse Nature Reserve 6G 43
Livery Dole Almshouses EX2: Exe . . .1C 26
Livonia Rd. EX10: Sidm 3D 38
Lloyds Ct. EX1: Whip 4G 13
Lloyds Cres. EX1: Whip 5G 13
Locarno Rd. EX4: Exe 2F 25
Lock Cl. EX10: Sidm 1C 38
Lockfield Ct. EX2: Alph 5H 25
Locksley Cl. EX2: Cou W 6E 27
Lockwood Ho. Camp Site
EX7: Daw 6C 46
Lockyer Av. EX10: Sidm 1E 39
Lodge Hill EX4: Exe 4G 11
Lodge Trad. Est. EX5: Broadc 1G 15
London Inn Sq. EX4: Exe 2E 5 (6B 12)
London Rd. EX5: Rock, Whim 2C 16
Longacres EX2: Exe 5G 5 (1B 26)
Longbrook La. EX8: Lymp 3A 42
Longbrook St. EX4: Exe 2E 5 (5A 12)
Longbrook Ter. EX4: Exe 1D 4 (5A 12)
Long Causeway EX8: Exmth 3D 48
Long Copp EX9: Bud S 3G 45
Longdogs Cl. EX11: Ott M 2E 21
Longdogs La. EX11: Ott M 2E 21
Longdown Rd. EX6: Long 4A 24
Longfield Est. EX6: Star 1E 47
Longfield Rd. EX6: Star 1E 47
Long La. EX8: Exmth 3E 49
Longmeadow EX5: Clyst M 3C 28
EX5: Wood 5G 35
Longmeadow Rd. EX8: Lymp 2B 42
Long Orchard EX5: Cranb 2A 16
Long Pk. EX5: Wood 5G 35
Lonsdale Rd. EX1: Heav 1E 27
Looe Rd. EX4: Exe 1A 4 (5G 11)
Lopes Hall EX4: Exe 3A 12
Loram Way EX2: Alph 6A 26
Lords Way EX2: Won 3G 27
Louisa Pl. EX8: Exmth 3C 48
Louisa Ter. EX8: Exmth 4C 48
Louvigny Cl. EX14: Fen 1H 9
Lovelace Cres. EX8: Exmth 1E 49
Lovelace Gdns. EX2: Alph 6H 25
Lovell Cl. EX8: Exmth 4E 43
Lovering Cl. EX8: Exmth 4E 43
Lowbrook EX5: Rock 3E 17
Lowena La. EX11: W Hill 4F 19
Lwr. Albert St. EX1: Exe 2G 5 (6B 12)
Lwr. Argyll Rd. EX4: Exe 3G 11
Lower Av. EX1: Heav 6D 12
Lower Barton EX5: Cranb 2B 16
Lwr. Brand La. EX14: Hon 5E 23
Lwr. Broad Oak Rd. EX11: W Hill 6G 19
Lower Budleigh EX9: E Bud 6D 40
Lwr. Cloister Wlk. EX6: Exmin 3H 31
(off Devington Pk.)
Lwr. Coombe St. EX1: Exe . . .5C 4 (1H 25)
Lwr. Duck St. EX6: Exmin 5B 32
Lower Farthings EX10: New P 2C 36
Lwr. Fore St. EX8: Exmth 3C 48
Lower Griggs EX10: Sidm 2F 39
Lwr. Halsdon La. EX8: Exmth 6B 42
Lwr. Harrington La. EX4: Pin 3A 14
Lwr. Hill Barton Rd.
EX1: Heav, Sow 6G 13
Lwr. King's Av. EX4: Exe 4B 12
Lower Knoll EX8: Exmth 3F 49
Lwr. Ladram La. EX9: Ott'n 4H 41
Lower La. EX3: Ebf 4A 34
Lwr. Marlpits Hill EX14: Hon 5F 23
Lwr. Northcote Rd. EX14: Hon 2G 23
Lwr. North St. EX4: Exe 2B 4 (6H 11)
Lwr. Rackclose La. EX1: Exe 4B 4
(off West St.)
Lower Rd. EX5: Wood S 1E 35
Lower St German's Rd. EX4: Exe 4A 12

Lwr. Shapter St. EX3: Top 4F 33
Lower Shillingford EX2: Shil A 2C 30
Lower Summerlands
EX1: Exe 2G 5 (6B 12)
Lower Way EX10: Harp 1E 37
LOWER WEAR 1B 32
Lwr. Wear Rd. EX2: Cou W 6E 27
Lower Wheathill EX10: Sidm 1D 38
(not continuous)
Lwr. Woodhayes Ct. EX5: Whim 5B 8
LOWER WOOLBROOK 3C 38
Lucas Av. EX4: Exe 4B 12
Luccombe La. EX2: Exe 3G 25
(off Alphington Rd.)
Lucky La. EX2: Exe 5D 4 (1A 26)
Lucombe Ct. EX4: Exe 5B 12
(off Stadium Way)
Ludwell La. EX2: Won 2E 27
Lumley Cl. EX6: Kenton 1B 46
Lustleigh Cl. EX2: Matf 6A 26
Lusways EX10: Sidm 5E 39
Luxtons Pk. EX11: Ott M 2C 20
Lydia Cl. EX10: New P 1B 36
Lymeborne Av. EX1: Heav 6E 13
Lymebourne Av. EX10: Sidm 3D 38
Lymebourne La. EX10: Sidm 3D 38
Lymebourne Pk. EX10: Sidm 3D 38
LYMPSTONE 2A 42
Lympstone Village Station (Rail) . . .2A 42
Lyncombe Cl. EX4: Exe 3C 12
Lyndhurst Rd. EX2: Exe 5H 5 (1C 26)
EX8: Exmth 1C 48
Lynwood Av. EX4: Exe 1G 25

M

Macauley Cl. EX14: Hon 3G 23
McCoys Arc. EX4: Exe 4B 4
Madagascar Cl. EX8: Exmth 1G 49
Maddocks Row EX4: Exe 2C 4 (6H 11)
Madeira Ct. EX8: Exmth 4D 48
Madeira Vs. EX8: Exmth 2C 48
Madeira Wlk. EX8: Exmth 4D 48
EX9: Bud S 5H 45
Madison Av. EX1: Heav 6E 13
Madison Wharf EX8: Exmth 3A 48
Maer Bay Ct. EX8: Exmth 4D 48
Maer La. EX8: Exmth, L'ham 4E 49
Maer Rd. EX8: Exmth 4E 49
Maer Va. EX8: Exmth 3E 49
Magdalen Bri. Ct. EX2: Exe 4E 5
Magdalen Cotts. EX1: Exe 4F 5 (1B 26)
Magdalen Gdns. EX2: Exe 4H 5 (1C 26)
Magdalen Rd. EX2: Exe 4F 5 (1B 26)
Magdalen St. EX2: Exe 4D 4 (1A 26)
Magnolia Av. EX2: Won 3E 27
EX8: Exmth 1G 49
Magnolia Cen. EX8: Exmth 3C 48
(off Chapel St.)
Magnolia Wlk. EX8: Exmth 3C 48
Magpie Cres. EX2: Exe 2D 24
Magpie La. EX14: Hon 6F 23
Main Rd. EX4: Pin 3A 14
EX6: Exmin 2A 32
(Sannerville Way)
EX6: Exmin 5C 32
(Station Rd.)
Majorfield Rd. EX3: Top 3F 33
Malden Cl. EX10: Sidm 2D 38
Malden La. EX10: Sidm 1D 38
Malden Rd. EX10: Sidm 1D 38
Mallard Rd. EX2: Sow 1A 28
Mallison Cl. EX4: Exe 4F 11
Malt Field EX8: Lymp 2B 42
Maltings, The EX2: Heav 1D 26
Malvern Gdns. EX2: Won 2E 27

Malvern Rd. EX10: Sidm 3C 38
Mamhead Bus. Units
EX2: Mar B 6B 26
Mamhead Rd. EX2: Won 2G 27
EX6: Kenton 2A 46
Mamhead Vw. EX8: Exmth 3A 48
Manaton Cl. EX2: Matf 6A 26
Manaton St. EX2: Matf 6A 26
Manchester Rd. EX8: Exmth 3B 48
Manchester St. EX8: Exmth 2B 48
Mandrake Cl. EX2: Alph 5H 25
Mandrake Rd. EX2: Alph 5G 25
Manley Cl. EX5: Whim 4A 8
Manna Ash Ct. EX2: Exe 6G 5
Manor Cl. EX10: Sidm 4C 38
EX14: Westo 4A 22
Manor Cres. EX14: Hon 5E 23
Manor Gdns. EX6: Kenton 1A 46
(off Slittercombe La.)
Manor Pk. EX5: Clyst M 3C 28
Manor Pavilion Theatre 6C 38
Manor Rd. EX4: Exe 1G 25
EX10: Sidm 6C 38
Mansell Copse Wlk. EX2: Won 2D 26
Mansfield Rd. EX4: Exe 4C 12
Mansfield Ter. EX9: Bud S 3H 45
Mansion House, The EX6: Exmin 3H 31
Manstone Av. EX10: Sidm 2C 38
(not continuous)
Manstone Cl. EX10: Sidm 1D 38
(not continuous)
Manstone La. EX10: Sidm 3D 38
Manstone Mead EX10: Sidm 1D 38
Manston Rd. EX1: Heav 5C 12
Manston Ter. EX2: Exe 1C 26
Manstree Rd. EX2: Shil G 4A 30
Manstree Ter. EX2: Shil G 4A 30
Maple Cl. EX14: Hon 6B 22
Maple Dr. EX8: Exmth 4F 43
Maple Rd. EX4: Exe 1F 25
EX5: Broadc 4F 7
Marcom Cl. EX8: Exmth 4F 43
Marcus Ho. EX4: Exe 1C 4
Marcus Rd. EX8: Exmth 6F 43
Mardon Hall EX4: Exe 3H 11
Mardon Hill EX4: Exe 3H 11
Margaret Cl. EX4: Whip 3G 13
Margaret Rd. EX4: Exe 3C 12
Margaret St. EX8: Exmth 3C 48
(off Chapel St.)
Marina Ct. EX8: Exmth 4D 48
Marine Ct. EX9: Bud S 5H 45
Marine Pde. EX9: Bud S 5H 45
Marine Way EX8: Exmth 2C 48
Marino, The EX10: Sidm 6B 38
Marions Way EX8: Exmth 5F 43
Maristow Av. EX8: Exmth 5D 42
Maritime Ct. EX2: Exe 6D 4 (2A 26)
Marker's Cottage 3F 7
Marker Way EX14: Hon 5E 23
Market Pl. EX10: Sidm 6D 38
Market Sq. EX4: Exe 3C 4
Market St. EX1: Exe 4C 4 (1H 25)
EX8: Exmth 3C 48
Markham La. EX2: Alph 1D 30
EX6: Ide, Shil A 6D 24
Marlborough Cl. EX8: Exmth 5G 43
Marlborough Ct. EX2: Matf 6A 26
Marlborough Dr. EX2: Won 1H 27
Marlborough Rd. EX2: Exe . . .5G 5 (1B 26)
Marles, The EX8: Exmth 5E 43
Marley Dr. EX8: Exmth 2F 43
Marley Hayes EX8: Exmth 2F 43
Marley Rd. EX8: Exmth 5D 42
Marlpits La. EX14: Hon 4E 23
Marpool Cres. EX8: Exmth 1E 49
Marpool Hill EX8: Exmth 2D 48

MARSH BARTON 4A 26
Marsh Barton Rd. EX2: Mar B 3H 25
Marsh Barton Trad. Est.
  EX2: Mar B 6C 26
                        (Exeter Trade Cen.)
  EX2: Mar B 4A 26
                        (Marsh Grn. Rd. E.)
MARSH GREEN 5A 18
Marsh Grn. Hill EX5: Mar G 5A 18
Marsh Grn. La. EX5: Mar G 5B 18
Marsh Grn. Rd. E. EX2: Mar B 4A 26
Marsh Grn. Rd. Nth. EX2: Mar B 3A 26
Marsh Grn. Rd. W.
  EX2: Alph, Mar B 4H 25
Marsh La. EX3: Clyst G 2G 33
Marshrow La. EX6: Exmin 6B 32
Martins La. EX1: Exe 3D 4 (6A 12)
Martins Rd. EX8: Exmth 5G 43
Marwood La. EX5: Ayle 6C 16
Marwood Pl. EX14: Hon 3F 23
                        (off Monkton Rd.)
Mary Arches St. EX4: Exe . . .3B 4 (6H 11)
Maryfield Av. EX4: Exe 4B 12
Marypole Rd. EX4: Exe 3D 12
Marypole Wlk. EX4: Exe 3D 12
Masefield Rd. EX4: Whip 4G 13
Masey Rd. EX8: Exmth 1F 49
Masterson St. EX2: Won 3D 26
MATFORD 6A 26
Matford (Park & Ride) 1F 31
Matford Av. EX2: Exe 6G 5 (2B 26)
Matford Bus. Pk. EX2: Mar B 6B 26
Matford Centre, The EX2: Matf 6B 26
Matford La. EX2: Exe 6F 5 (2B 26)
Matford M. EX2: Matf 1G 31
Matford Pk. Rd. EX2: Matf 5A 26
Matford Rd. EX2: Exe 6G 5 (2B 26)
Mathews Cl. EX14: Hon 5D 22
Matthews Ct. EX4: Pin 2H 13
Maunder's Hill EX9: Ott'n 4G 41
Maunders Pl. EX9: Ott'n 4G 41
Mayfield Dr. EX8: Exmth 3F 49
Mayfield Rd. EX2: Won 1E 27
  EX4: Pin 3A 14
Mayfield Way EX5: Cranb 2A 16
Mayflower Av. EX4: Exe 2B 12
May St. EX4: Exe 5B 12
May Ter. EX10: Sidm 5D 38
Mead Cotts. EX8: L'ham 2H 49
Mead Cross EX5: Cranb 2A 16
Meadhurst Ct. EX10: Sidm 5C 38
Meadowbrook Cl. EX4: Exe 4E 11
Meadow Cl. EX5: Clyst M 3G 29
  EX8: Lymp 2B 42
  EX9: Bud S 4F 45
  EX11: Ott M 1E 21
Meadow Dr. EX10: New P 1D 36
Meadow La. EX5: Cranb 2A 16
  EX9: Bud S 4G 45
Meadow Rd. EX9: Bud S 4F 45
Meadows Cres. EX14: Hon 4E 23
Meadow St. EX8: Exmth 2C 48
Meadow Vw. EX8: Lymp 2B 42
Meadow Vw. Cl. EX10: Sidm 4E 39
Meadow Vw. Rd. EX8: Exmth 5G 43
Meadow Way EX2: Heav 1D 26
  EX10: Col R 6B 36
Mead Vw. Rd. EX14: Hon 4E 23
Meadway EX10: Sidm 3D 38
Mecca Bingo
  Exeter .3C 4
Mede, The EX3: Top 3E 33
  EX4: Whip 4F 13
Medley Ct. EX4: Exe 4E 11
Meeting La. EX8: Lymp 1A 42
Meeting St. EX8: Exmth 2C 48
Meetways La. EX8: Exmth 3F 49

Melbourne Ct. EX2: Exe 5E 5
Melbourne Pl. EX2: Exe 5E 5 (1A 26)
Melbourne St.
  EX2: Exe 6E 5 (2A 26)
Meldon Ct. EX9: Bud S 4H 45
Membury Cl. EX1: Sow 6H 13
Mercer Ct. EX2: Cou W 4E 27
Meresyke EX8: Exmth 3E 49
Merlin Bus. Pk. EX5: Clyst H 6B 16
Merlin Cres. EX4: Whip 3E 13
Mermaid Cl. EX1: Exe 4C 4
Mermaid Yd. EX1: Exe 4C 4 (1H 25)
Merrion Av. EX8: Exmth 3F 49
Merrivale Rd. EX4: Exe 2F 25
Meteorological Office 5H 13
Meyer Ct. EX2: Heav 1E 27
Michael Browning Way
  EX2: Exe 6D 4 (2A 26)
Michigan Way EX4: Exe 2A 12
MIDDLE MOOR 2H 27
Middle St. EX9: E Bud 5D 40
Middletown La. EX9: E Bud 5D 40
MIDDLEWOOD 3E 47
Middlewood Hill EX6: Cockw 4E 47
MIDDLE WOOLBROOK 2C 38
Midway EX8: Exmth 1G 49
Midway Cl. EX2: Alph 5G 25
Midway Ter. EX2: Alph 5G 25
Milbury Cl. EX6: Exmin 3A 32
Milbury La. EX6: Exmin 4B 32
Mildmay Cl. EX4: Exe 5F 11
Mile Gdns. EX4: Whip 2D 12
Mile La. EX4: Whip 1D 12
Mill, The EX2: Exe 2B 26
Millbrook La. EX2: Exe 4C 26
Millcroft EX11: Ott M 2D 20
Milldale Cres. EX14: Hon 4D 22
Mill Dr. EX2: Cou W 5D 26
Miller Cl. EX2: Won 2G 27
Millers Way EX14: Hon 4D 22
Miller Way EX6: Exmin 3H 31
Milletts Cl. EX6: Exmin 4A 32
Millford Av. EX10: Sidm 5D 38
Millford Rd. EX10: Sidm 5D 38
Millhead Rd. EX14: Hon 4D 22
Millin Way EX7: Daw W 6E 47
Mill La. EX2: Alph 5H 25
  EX2: Cou W 5D 26
                        (not continuous)
  EX3: Exton 6A 34
  EX5: Broadc 3E 15
  EX10: New P 3C 36
Millmoor La. EX10: New P 1D 36
Millmoor Va. EX10: New P 1D 36
Mill Pk. Ind. Est. EX5: Wood S 1H 35
Mill Rd. EX2: Cou W 5D 26
Mill Stream Ct. EX11: Ott M 2C 20
Mill St. EX10: Sidm 5D 38
  EX11: Ott M 2D 20
  EX14: Hon 4D 22
Milltown La. EX10: Sidm 3E 39
Mill Yd. EX2: Cou W 5D 26
Milton Cl. EX8: Exmth 3E 43
Milton Rd. EX2: Won 3D 26
Mincinglake Rd. EX4: Exe 3C 12
Minifie Rd. EX14: Hon 3D 22
Minster Rd. EX6: Exmin 3B 32
Mint, The EX4: Exe 3B 4 (1H 25)
Mirey La. EX5: Wood 5G 35
Mission Ct. EX4: Exe 5B 4
Mitre La. EX4: Exe 3B 4 (6H 11)
Modred Ct. EX4: Whip 3E 13
Monitor Cl. EX2: Exe 2H 25
MONKERTON 4A 14
Monkerton Ct. EX1: Pin 4A 14
Monkerton Dr. EX1: Pin 4A 14
Monkey La. EX10: New P 3B 36

Monk's Rd. EX4: Exe 5C 12
Monkswell Rd. EX4: Exe 4C 12
Monkton Rd. EX14: Hon, Monk 3F 23
                        (not continuous)
Monmouth Av. EX3: Top 4F 33
Monmouth Hill EX3: Top 4F 33
Monmouth St. EX3: Top 4F 33
Monmouth Way EX14: Hon 4F 23
Montague Gdns. EX9: Bud S 4E 45
Montague Ri. EX4: Exe 5A 12
Monterey EX8: Exmth 4E 49
Monterey Gdns. EX4: Exe 3C 12
Montgomery Rd. EX2: Won 1H 27
                        (off Sidmouth Rd.)
Mont Le Grand EX1: Heav 6C 12
Montpelier Ct.
  EX4: Exe 1A 4 (5G 11)
Montpellier Ct. EX8: Exmth 3D 48
                        (off Montpellier Rd.)
Montpellier Rd. EX8: Exmth 3C 48
Moonhill Cl. EX2: Alph 6A 26
Moon Ridge EX2: Alph 1C 32
Moorcourt Cl. EX10: Sidm 6B 38
Mooredge La. EX5: Broadc 1D 6
Moorfield Cl. EX8: Exmth 1E 49
Moorfield Rd. EX8: Exmth 1D 48
Moorhaven EX9: Bud S 3F 45
Moorhayes Ct. EX5: Tala 1E 9
Moorings, The EX8: Exmth 3A 48
Moorlands EX11: W Hill 4F 19
Moorlands Rd. EX9: Bud S 4D 44
Moorland Way EX4: Exe 4E 11
Moor La. EX2: Sow 6A 14
  EX4: Polt 3B 6
  EX5: Broadc 1E 7
  EX5: Clyst M, Wood S 3C 34
  EX9: Bud S 3F 45
Moormead EX9: Bud S 4F 45
Moor Pk. EX8: Exmth 3E 49
  EX14: Hon 6D 22
Moor Pk. La. EX10: Sidm 4H 37
Moor Vw. Cl. EX10: Sidm 2B 38
Moorview Cl. EX4: Exe 3B 12
Morgan Ct. EX8: Exmth 3C 48
                        (off Rolle Rd.)
Morley Rd. EX4: Exe 4C 12
Mortimer Ct. EX2: Cou W 4E 27
                        (not continuous)
Morton Cres. EX8: Exmth 3B 48
Morton Cres. M. EX8: Exmth 3B 48
Morton Rd. EX8: Exmth 3B 48
Morven Dr. EX8: Exmth 5C 42
Mosshayne La. EX1: W Cly 1C 14
  EX5: Clyst H 2E 15
Mossop Cl. EX11: Ott M 2D 20
Mountain Cl. EX8: Exmth 1H 49
Mountbatten Cl. EX8: Exmth 5F 43
Mount Cl. EX14: Hon 4D 22
MOUNT DINHAM 3B 4 (6H 11)
Mt. Dinham Ct. EX4: Exe 2B 4 (6H 11)
Mount Howe EX3: Top 4G 33
Mt. Pleasant Av. EX8: Exmth 4D 42
Mt. Pleasant Ct. EX8: Exmth 5D 42
Mt. Pleasant Rd. EX4: Exe 4C 12
MOUNT RADFORD 4F 5 (1B 26)
Mt. Radford Cres.
  EX2: Exe 5F 5 (1B 26)
Mt. Radford Sq. EX2: Exe 5F 5
Mount Vw. EX14: Fen 1H 9
Mt. Wear Sq. EX2: Cou W 6F 27
Mowbray Av. EX4: Exe 1E 5 (5A 12)
Mowbray Ct. EX2: Won 1E 27
Mowlish La. EX6: Kenton 3A 46
Mudbank La. EX8: Exmth 6B 42
Mulberry Cl. EX1: Whip 6F 13
Musgrave Ho. EX4: Exe 2D 4
                        (off Musgrave Row)

Musgrave Row EX4: Exe 2D **4** (6A **12**)
Mushroom Rd. EX5: Clyst M 4H **29**
Muttersmoor Rd. EX10: Sidm 3H **37**
Mutton La. EX2: Alph, Matf 6A **26**
Myrtle Cl. EX2: Alph 5H **25**
Myrtle Rd. EX4: Exe 2E **25**
Myrtle Row EX8: Exmth 3C **48**

N

Nadder Bottom EX4: Hals, Nad 4A **10**
Nadder La. EX4: Nad 4B **10**
Nadder Pk. Rd. EX4: Exe 1D **24**
NADDERWATER 5B **10**
Napier Ter. EX4: Exe 3B **4** (6H **11**)
Naps La. EX10: Col R 3A **36**
Nash Gro. EX4: Exe 3G **11**
Nasmith Cl. EX8: Exmth 6F **43**
Needlewood Cl. EX11: W Hill 6E **19**
Nelson Cl. EX3: Top 3E **33**
Nelson Dr. EX8: Exmth 1G **49**
Nelson Rd. EX4: Exe 5A **4** (2G **25**)
Nelson Way EX2: Won 1G **27**
Newbery Commercial Cen.
  EX5: Clyst H 6B **16**
New Bridge St. EX4: Exe 5B **4** (1H **25**)
New Bldgs. *EX4: Exe* *4B 12*
  (off Well St.)
  EX5: Broadc 3E **7**
Newcombe St. EX1: Heav 6D **12**
Newcombe St. Gdns. EX1: Heav 6E **13**
Newcombe Ter. *EX1: Heav* *6D 12*
  (off Newcombe St.)
Newcourt Rd. EX3: Top 6A **28**
Newcourt Way EX2: Cou W 4H **27**
Newfoundland Cl. EX4: Exe 2C **12**
Newhayes Cl. EX2: Exe 4G **25**
Newlands EX14: Hon 3E **23**
Newlands Av. EX8: Exmth 1F **49**
Newlands Cl. EX2: Exe 4G **25**
  EX10: Sidm 1D **38**
Newlands Rd. EX10: Sidm 1D **38**
New La. EX11: Ott M 1E **21**
Newman Ct. EX4: Exe 1E **25**
Newman Rd. EX4: Exe 2E **25**
New North Rd. EX4: Exe 1B **4** (4G **11**)
  EX8: Exmth 2C **48**
Newport Pk. EX2: Cou W 1C **32**
Newport Rd. EX2: Cou W 1C **32**
New Rd. EX5: Rock 3D **18**
  EX6: Star 2E **47**
New St. EX8: Exmth 2C **48**
  EX10: Sidm 6D **38**
  EX11: Ott M 1E **21**
  EX14: Hon 3E **23**
Newton Cen. EX2: Mar B 6C **26**
NEWTON POPPLEFORD 1D **36**
NEW TOWN 5D **38**
NEWTOWN 2H **5** (6C **12**)
Newtown EX10: Sidm 5D **38**
Newtown Cl. EX1: Exe 2G **5**
New Valley Rd. EX4: Exe 5F **11**
New Way EX5: Wood S 2G **35**
New Way Bldgs. EX8: Exmth 2C **48**
NHS WALK-IN CENTRE
  Exeter - Sidwell Street 2E **5**
  Exeter - Wonford 2D **26**
Nicholas Cen. EX1: Exe 1H **5** (5C **12**)
Nicholas Rd. EX1: Heav 6E **13**
Nichols Way EX1: Exe 1H **5** (5C **12**)
Nightingale Wlk. EX2: Exe 3D **24**
Nineteen Steps *EX9: Bud S* *5H 45*
  (off Madeira Wlk.)
Norman Cl. EX8: Exmth 5F **43**
Norman Ct. EX2: Matf 5A **26**
Norman Cres. EX9: Bud S 3F **45**

Normandy Cl. EX8: Exmth 6G **43**
Normandy Rd. EX1: Heav 6D **12**
Norman Lockyer Observatory 4F **39**
Norman M. EX2: Sow 2H **27**
Norman Pl. EX2: Sow 2H **27**
Norman Stevens Cl. EX8: Exmth 3E **49**
North Av. EX1: Heav 2H **5** (6C **12**)
North Bri. Pl. EX4: Exe 2B **4** (6H **11**)
Northbrook Cl. EX4: Whip 3E **13**
Northbrook Golf Course 4D **26**
NORTHCOTE 1H **23**
Northcote Hill EX14: Hon 2G **23**
Northcote La. EX14: Hon 3D **22**
Northcote Rd. EX14: Hon 2G **23**
Northcott Theatre 3H **11**
Northernhay Gdns. 1D **4** (5H **11**)
Northernhay Ga.
  EX4: Exe 2C **4** (6H **11**)
Northernhay Pl. EX4: Exe 2D **4** (6A **12**)
Northernhay Sq. EX4: Exe 2C **4** (6H **11**)
Northernhay St.
  EX4: Exe 3C **4** (6H **11**)
Northfield EX4: Exe 4G **11**
North Ga. Ho. EX4: Exe 2C **4**
North Grange EX2: Sow 3H **27**
Nth. Lawn Ct. EX1: Heav 6D **12**
Northleigh Hill Rd.
  EX14: Hon, Offw 6G **23**
NORTHMOSTOWN 2E **37**
North Pk. Almshouses EX1: Exe 4F **5**
North Pk. Rd. EX4: Exe 3H **11**
North St. EX1: Heav 6D **12**
  EX3: Top 4F **33**
  EX4: Exe 3C **4** (6H **11**)
  EX8: Exmth 2C **48**
  EX11: Ott M 1E **21**
Northview Rd. EX9: Bud S 5F **45**
Norton Pl. EX8: Exmth 1G **49**
Norwich Cl. EX8: Exmth 3F **43**
Norwich Rd. EX4: Exe 6E **11**
Norwood Av. EX2: Exe 2B **26**
Norwood Ho. EX4: Exe 5A **12**
Nurseries Cl. EX3: Exton 6A **34**
  EX3: Top 2E **33**
Nursery Cl. EX8: Exmth 1E **49**
Nursery M. EX8: Exmth 1E **49**
Nutbrook EX8: Exmth 6D **42**
Nutwell Rd. EX8: Lymp 1A **42**

O

Oakbeer Orchard EX5: Cranb 2A **16**
Oak Bus. Units EX12: Mar B 6C **26**
Oak Cl. EX2: Shil A 2C **30**
  EX4: Pin .3A **14**
  EX6: Exmin 4A **32**
  EX11: Ott M 3D **20**
Oakfield Rd. EX4: Exe 5A **4** (1G **25**)
Oakfield St. EX1: Heav 1D **26**
Oakhayes Rd. EX5: Wood 5F **35**
Oak Hill EX9: E Bud 5E **41**
Oakhill EX9: E Bud 5D **40**
Oaklea EX14: Hon 3D **22**
Oakleigh Rd. EX8: Exmth 2D **48**
Oakley Cl. EX1: Pin 3A **14**
Oakley Wlk. EX5: Clyst M 3G **29**
Oak Meadow Golf Course 2E **47**
Oak Ridge EX2: Alph 6G **25**
Oak Rd. EX4: Exe 2F **25**
  EX5: Ayle 6D **18**
  EX11: High M 6D **18**
Oak Tree Cl. EX5: Broadc 4F **7**
Oaktree Cl. EX8: Exmth 4D **42**
Oak Tree Pl. EX2: Matf 6A **26**
Oak Tree Sq. EX10: Sidm 2C **38**
Oaktree Vs. EX10: New P 1D **36**

Oak Vw. EX14: Hon 5C **22**
Oakwood Ri. EX8: Exmth 4G **43**
Oberon Rd. EX1: Sow 5A **14**
Odeon Cinema
  Exeter 1F **5**
Odhams Wharf EX3: Ebf 3H **33**
Oil Mill La. EX5: Clyst M 4E **29**
Oil Mill Rd. EX5: Clyst M 4E **29**
Old Abbey Ct. EX2: Exe 3C **26**
Old Bakery Cl. EX4: Exe 5F **11**
Old Bystock Dr. EX8: Exmth 4G **43**
Old Coach La. EX1: Heav 6C **12**
Old Coach Rd. EX5: Broadc 4E **7**
Old Court House, The
  EX5: Wood 5F **35**
Old Dawlish Rd. EX6: Kennf 6D **30**
Old Ebford La. EX3: Ebf 4A **34**
Old Elm Rd. EX14: Hon 5B **22**
Old Farm Bungs. EX10: Sidm 2D **38**
Oldfields EX8: Exmth 3E **49**
Old Fore St. EX10: Sidm 6D **38**
Old Garden Pasture EX5: Cranb 2A **16**
Old Ide Cl. EX2: Ide 4E **25**
Old Ide La. EX2: Ide 4E **25**
Old Market Cl. EX2: Exe 3H **25**
Old Matford La. EX2: Matf 1F **31**
Old Mill Cl. EX2: Exe 6E **5** (2B **26**)
Old Nursery Dr. EX4: Whip 4F **13**
Old Okehampton Rd.
  EX4: Nad, Whip 5A **10**
Old Park Rd. EX4: Exe 1E **5** (5A **12**)
Old Pavilion Cl. EX2: Won 2G **27**
Old Pinn La. EX1: Pin 3A **14**
Old Rydon Cl. EX2: Cou W 4A **28**
Old Rydon La. EX2: Cou W 5G **27**
Old Rydon Ley EX2: Cou W 4H **27**
Old Saddlery, The *EX14: Hon* *3E 23*
  (off Queen St.)
Old Sawmills, The EX10: Col R 5A **36**
Old School Ct. *EX3: Top* *3F 33*
  (off Majorfield Rd.)
  EX14: Hon 3E **23**
Old Sludge Beds Nature Reserve . .2C **32**
Old's Vw. EX4: Exe 5G **11**
Old Tiverton Rd.
  EX4: Exe 1G **5** (5B **12**)
Old Vicarage Cl. EX2: Ide 5D **24**
Old Vicarage Rd. EX2: Exe 2G **25**
Olga Ter. EX8: Lymp 2B **42**
Omaha Dr. EX2: Cou W 5H **27**
Omega Centre, The EX2: Sow 6A **14**
Orangery, The *EX6: Exmin* *3H 31*
  (off Devington Pk.)
Orchard, The EX14: Hon 4D **22**
  (Mill St.)
  EX14: Hon 2H **23**
  (Tunnel La.)
Orchard Cl. EX1: Pin 3B **14**
  EX5: Wood 5G **35**
  EX8: Exmth 6D **42**
  EX8: Lymp 2A **42**
  EX9: E Bud 5D **40**
  EX10: New P 1B **36**
  EX10: Sidf 1E **39**
  EX10: Sidm 6B **38**
  EX11: Ott M 2E **21**
Orchard Ct. EX2: Sow 6A **14**
  EX5: Whim 4A **8**
Orchard Dr. EX9: Ott'n 4G **41**
Orchard Gdns. EX4: Exe 2F **25**
  EX5: Broadc 4F **7**
Orchard Hill EX2: Exe 3E **25**

Orchard La. EX6: E'don 5E 47
Orchardside EX10: Sidm 2D 38
Orchard Vw. EX1: Heav 1D 36
Orchard Way EX3: Top 3E 33
  EX6: Kenton 1A 46
  EX14: Hon 3F 23
          (not continuous)
Orcombe Ct. EX8: Exmth 1F 49
Oriole Dr. EX4: Exe 3B 12
Orwell Gth. EX4: Whip 4G 13
Osprey Rd. EX2: Sow 6B 14
Otago Cotts. EX2: Exe 3C 26
Otterbourne Ct. *EX9: Bud S* 5H 45
     (off Coastguard Rd.)
Otter Cl. EX11: W Hill 5F 19
Otter Ct. EX2: Matf 6A 26
  EX9: Bud S 4H 45
Otter Reach EX10: New P 1D 36
Otters Reach EX9: Bud S 3H 45
OTTERTON 4G 41
Otterton Mill 4F 41
Ottervale Rd. EX9: Bud S 4H 45
Otter Valley Pk. EX14: Hon 1H 23
Otter Vw. *EX11: Ott M* 2D 20
    (off St Saviours Rd.)
Ottery Moor EX14: Hon 3D 22
Ottery Moor La. EX14: Hon 3C 22
Ottery Rd. EX14: Fen 1H 9
OTTERY ST MARY 2D 20
OTTERY ST MARY HOSPITAL 2B 20
Ottery St Mary Leisure Cen. 2B 20
Ottery St. EX9: Ott'n 4G 41
Outer Ting Tong EX9: Know 2B 44
Oval Grn. *EX2: Won* 3G 27
    (off Woodwater La.)
Oxford Cl. EX8: Exmth 3G 43
Oxford Rd. EX4: Exe 1F 5 (5B 12)
Oxford St. EX2: Exe 6A 4 (2G 25)

P

Packhorse Cl. EX10: Sidf 1F 39
Paddock, The EX5: Whim 6B 8
Painters Ct. EX2: Exe 6C 4 (2H 25)
Palace Cotts. *EX8: Exmth* 2C 48
     (off Parade)
Palace Ga. EX1: Exe 3D 4 (1A 26)
Pale Gate Cl. EX14: Hon 2F 23
Palm Cl. EX8: Exmth 4F 43
Palmer Ct. EX9: Bud S 4G 45
Palmer M. *EX9: Bud S* 5G 45
    (off Victoria Pl.)
Palmer's La. EX5: Mar G 4B 18
Palmerston Dr. EX4: Exe 5E 11
Pamela Rd. EX1: Heav 5D 12
Pancras Sq. EX4: Exe 3C 4
Pankhurst Cl. EX8: L'ham 2G 49
Panney, The EX4: Exe 5E 13
Parade EX8: Exmth 2C 48
Paris St. EX1: Exe 2E 5 (6A 12)
Park & Ride
  Digby 3H 27
  Honiton Road 6A 14
  Matford 1F 31
  Sowton 2A 28
Park Cl. EX5: Wood 6G 35
Park Ct. EX14: Hon 5B 22
Parkers Cross La. EX1: Pin 2B 14
Parker's Rd. EX6: Star 2E 47
Parkfield Rd. EX3: Top 3F 33
Parkfield Way EX3: Top 3F 33
Park Five Bus. Cen.
  EX2: Sow 2A 28
Parkhayes EX5: Wood S 1G 35
Parkhouse Rd. EX2: Exe 3F 25
Parkland Dr. EX2: Won 3G 27

Park La. EX4: Pin 1H 13
  EX8: Exmth 1C 48
  EX9: Bud S 4F 45
  EX9: Ott'n 5G 41
Park Pl. EX1: Heav 6D 12
  EX2: Exe 5G 5 (1B 26)
Park Rd. EX1: Heav 1H 5 (5C 12)
  EX8: Exmth 1C 48
Parkside Ct. EX2: Exe 4E 5
Parkside Cres. EX1: W Cly 1B 14
Parkside Dr. EX8: Exmth 5F 43
Parkside Rd. EX1: W Cly 1B 14
Parks La. EX9: Bud S 5H 45
Park Vw. EX4: Exe 2G 25
  EX6: Kenton 1C 46
  EX8: Lymp 2C 42
Park Way EX8: Exmth 1E 49
     (not continuous)
Parkway EX2: Exe 3F 25
  EX5: Wood 6G 35
Parliament St. EX4: Exe 3C 4 (6H 11)
Parr Cl. EX1: Exe 1G 5 (5B 12)
Parr St. EX1: Exe 1G 5 (5B 12)
Parrys Farm Cl. EX8: Exmth 5E 43
Parsonage La. EX14: Hon 4F 23
Parsonage Way EX5: Wood 5G 35
Parson Cl. EX8: Exmth 5E 43
Parsons Cl. EX10: New P 2B 36
Parsons La. EX5: Rock 3B 16
Parsons Path *EX3: Top* 3F 33
    (off Monmouth Av.)
Parthia Pl. EX8: Exmth 6G 43
Partridge Rd. EX8: Exmth 4E 43
Passaford La. EX10: N'town 5E 37
Paternoster Row EX11: Ott M 1D 20
Pathworlands EX10: Sidm 3C 38
Patricia Cl. EX4: Exe 2A 12
Patteson Dr. EX11: Ott M 1F 21
Paul St. EX4: Exe 3C 4 (6H 11)
Pauntley Gdns. EX10: Sidm 6B 38
Pavilion Pl. EX2: Exe 4E 5 (1A 26)
Paxford Ho. Sq. EX11: Ott M 1D 20
Paynes Ct. EX4: Whip 4F 13
Peacock Pl. EX6: Star 1F 47
Peak Hill Rd. EX10: Sidm 6G 37
Pear Tree Cl. EX6: Kenton 1B 46
Peaslands Rd. EX10: Sidm 4C 38
Pebble La. EX9: Bud S 5G 45
Peel Row EX4: Whip 4G 13
Peep La. EX4: Exe 2A 4 (6G 11)
Pegasus Ct. EX1: Heav 6D 12
Pellinore Rd. EX4: Whip 3E 13
Pencarwick Ho. EX8: Exmth 4C 48
Pendeen Ct. EX8: Exmth 2F 49
Pendragon Rd. EX4: Whip 2D 12
Penhayes Cl. EX6: Kenton 1B 46
Penhayes Rd. EX6: Kenton 1B 46
Peninsula Pk. EX2: Won 2G 27
Penitentiary Ct. EX2: Exe 5D 4 (1A 26)
Penlee EX9: Bud S 5G 45
Penleonard Cl. EX2: Exe 5H 5 (1C 26)
Pennant Ho. *EX8: Exmth* 3A 48
     (off Shelly Rd.)
PENNSYLVANIA 3B 12
Pennsylvania Cl. EX4: Exe 4B 12
Pennsylvania Ct. EX4: Exe 4B 12
Pennsylvania Cres. EX4: Exe 4A 12
Pennsylvania Pk. EX4: Exe 3B 12
Pennsylvania Rd. EX4: Exe 1A 12
Penny Cl. EX6: Exmin 4A 32
Pentgrove Ct. EX8: Exmth 2F 49
Perceval Rd. EX4: Whip 3E 13
Percy Rd. EX2: Exe 3H 25
Perriam's Pl. EX9: Bud S 4G 45
Perridge Cl. EX2: Exe 3E 25
Perriman's Row EX8: Exmth 2C 48
Perrin Way EX4: Pin 3H 13

Perry Rd. EX4: Exe 4H 11
Perrys Gdns. EX11: W Hill 5F 19
Perth Cl. EX4: Exe 2C 12
Peryam Cres. EX2: Won 2E 27
Peterborough Rd. EX4: Exe 5E 11
Phear Av. EX8: Exmth 2D 48
Phear Park 1D 48
Philip Ho. EX2: Sow 6A 14
Philip Rd. EX4: Exe 4D 12
Phillipps Av. EX8: Exmth 6D 42
Phillips Sq. EX14: Hon 3D 22
Piazza Terracina EX2: Exe 6D 4
Piccadilly La. *EX11: Ott M* 2D 20
     (off Mill St.)
Pickwick Arc. EX4: Exe 4C 4
Pier Head EX8: Exmth 3A 48
Pilgrim Ho. EX4: Exe 4D 12
Pilot Wharf *EX8: Exmth* 3A 48
     (off Pier Head)
Pilton La. EX1: Pin 4H 13
Pinaster Cl. EX14: Hon 4G 23
Pinbridge Ct. *EX1: Pin* 4A 14
     (off Old Pinn La.)
Pinbridge M. EX4: Pin 3H 13
Pinbrook Ind. Est. EX4: Pin 3H 13
Pinbrook M. EX4: Pin 2G 13
Pinbrook Rd. EX4: Pin 3H 13
Pinbrook Units EX4: Pin 3H 13
Pinces Cotts. EX2: Exe 3G 25
Pinces Gdns. EX2: Exe 3G 25
Pinces Rd. EX2: Exe 3G 25
Pine Av. EX4: Exe 5F 11
Pinefields Cl. EX11: W Hill 6G 19
Pine Gdns. EX14: Hon 3F 23
Pine Gro. EX14: Hon 3F 23
Pine Pk. Rd. EX14: Hon 4F 23
Pineridge Cl. EX4: Exe 2F 25
Pines, The EX4: Exe 5F 11
  EX14: Hon 4F 23
Pines Rd. EX8: Exmth 4E 43
Pine Vw. Cl. EX8: Exmth 5H 43
PINHOE 2A 14
Pinhoe Rd. EX4: Exe, Pin, Whip ..5C 12
Pinhoe Station (Rail) 3A 14
Pinhoe Trad. Est. EX4: Exe 3H 13
Pinncourt La. EX1: Pin 2B 14
Pinn Hill EX1: Pin 2B 14
Pinn La. EX1: Pin 3A 14
  EX10: N'town, Sidm 2H 41
Pinn Valley Rd. EX1: Pin 3B 14
Pinwood La. EX4: Whip 2F 13
     (not continuous)
Pinwood Mdw. Dr. EX4: Whip 2F 13
Pippin Cl. EX1: Heav 6G 13
Piscombe La. EX9: Ott'n 4H 41
Pitson La. EX10: N'town 4E 37
Pitt Hill EX6: Kenton 1A 46
Pitt Pk. EX5: Cranb 2B 16
Pitts Ct. EX2: Exe 2B 26
Plantagenet Wlk. *EX2: Sow* 2H 27
     (off Heraldry Way)
Plassey Cl. EX4: Exe 2B 12
Playmoor Dr. EX1: Pin 3B 14
Plume of Feathers Cl. EX11: Ott M ..1E 21
Plumtree Dr. EX2: Won 2F 27
Plumtree La. EX5: Whim 6B 8
POCOMBE BRIDGE 3D 24
Pocombe Hill EX2: Exe 3D 24
Point Exe EX4: Exe 1A 4 (5G 11)
Point Ter. EX8: Exmth 3A 48
Polehouse La. EX2: Ide 6E 25
POLSLOE BRIDGE 5E 13
Polsloe Bridge Station (Rail) ...5E 13
POLSLOE PARK 1H 5 (5C 12)
POLSLOE PRIORY 4D 12
Polsloe Rd. EX1: Exe 1H 5 (5C 12)
POLTIMORE 4B 6

Poltimore Ct. EX4: Polt 3B **6**
Poltimore Sq. EX4: Exe 1E **5** (5A **12**)
Pooh Cottage Holiday Pk.
 EX9: Know 2E **45**
Poplar Cl. EX2: Exe 3G **25**
 EX8: Exmth 4F **43**
Poplar Row EX9: Bud S 5H **45**
Poplars, The EX4: Pin 2A **14**
Poplars Wlk. *EX5: Clyst M* *4F **29***
 (off Hazelmead Rd.)
Poppy Cl. EX4: Exe 4D **10**
Porchester Hgts. *EX4: Exe* *1F **5***
 (off Acland Rd.)
Portland Av. EX8: Exmth 3D **48**
Portland St. EX1: Exe 1G **5** (6C **12**)
Port Mer Cl. EX8: Exmth 4G **43**
Port Rd. EX6: Daw 5A **46**
 EX7: Daw 5A **46**
Post Coach Way EX5: Cranb 2B **16**
Potters Cl. EX11: W Hill 4F **19**
Pottery Cl. EX14: Hon 3F **23**
Pottles Cl. EX6: Exmin 5A **32**
Pouncel La. EX5: Cranb 2B **16**
Pound Cl. EX3: Top 2E **33**
 EX8: Exmth 6E **43**
Pound La. EX3: Top 2E **33**
 EX5: Wood 5G **35**
 EX8: Exmth 5D **42**
 EX10: Col R 4A **36**
Pound La. Trad. Est. EX8: Exmth . . .6E **43**
Poundsland EX5: Broadc 4E **7**
Pound St. EX8: Exmth 3C **48**
Powderham Castle 1C **46**
Powderham Cl. EX3: Top 2E **33**
Powderham Cres. EX4: Exe 4B **12**
Powderham Rd. EX2: Exe 2G **25**
Powderham Wlk. EX6: Exmin 3H **31**
Powhay Mills EX4: Exe 4A **4** (1H **25**)
Powlesland Rd. EX2: Alph 5H **25**
Powys Ho. EX10: Sidm 5C **38**
Prattshayes Farm Camp Site
 EX8: Exmth 3G **49**
Premier Pl. EX2: Exe 5G **5** (1B **26**)
Prescot Rd. EX4: Exe 1E **25**
Preston St. EX1: Exe 4C **4** (1H **25**)
Pretoria Rd. EX1: Heav 5C **12**
Priddis Cl. EX8: Exmth 4E **43**
Pridhams Way EX6: Exmin 4A **32**
Priestley Av. EX4: Whip 4F **13**
Primley Gdns. EX10: Sidm 2E **39**
Primley Mead EX10: Sidm 2E **39**
Primley Paddock EX10: Sidm 2D **38**
Primley Rd. EX10: Sidm 2D **38**
 (not continuous)
Primrose Lawn EX4: Exe 4D **10**
Prince Charles Cl. EX8: Exmth 6G **43**
Prince Charles Rd. EX4: Exe 4C **12**
Prince of Wales Dr. EX8: Exmth 1F **49**
Prince of Wales Rd. EX4: Exe 4H **11**
Princesshay EX1: Exe 2D **4** (6A **12**)
Princesshay Garden Apartments
 EX1: Exe *2E **5***
 (off Dix's Field)
Princesshay La. EX1: Exe 2E **5**
Princesshay Sq. EX1: Exe 3D **4**
Prince's Sq. EX2: Exe 2G **25**
Prince's St. E. EX2: Exe 3G **25**
Prince's St. Nth. EX2: Exe 2G **25**
Prince's St. Sth. EX2: Exe 3G **25**
Prince's St. W. EX2: Exe 2G **25**
Priory, The *EX6: Exmin* *3H **31***
 (off Devington Pk.)
Priory Cl. EX9: E Bud 4D **40**
Priory Gdns. EX4: Exe 4B **4**
Priory Rd. EX4: Exe 4C **12**
Priory Vw. EX4: Whip 4E **13**
Prison Cl. EX4: Exe 1D **4** (5A **12**)

Prospect Gdns. EX4: Exe 5C **12**
Prospect Pk. EX4: Exe 4B **12**
Prospect Pl. EX4: Exe 2G **25**
 EX10: Sidm *6D **38***
 (off Kings La.)
 EX11: Ott M 2D **20**
Puckridge Rd. EX4: Pin 2H **13**
Puffin Way EX2: Exe 3D **24**
Pulling Rd. EX4: Pin 2H **13**
Pulpit Wlk. EX2: Alph 1E **31**
Purcell Cl. EX2: Won 1G **27**
Pye Cnr. EX6: Kennf 6D **30**
Pynes Cl. EX9: E Bud 5D **40**
Pynes Hill EX2: Cou W 4F **27**
Pynes Hill Bus. Pk. EX2: Cou W 4G **27**
Pyramids Swimming and
 Leisure Centre, The 2F **5** (6B **12**)
Pytte Gdns. EX3: Clyst G 1A **34**

Q

Quadrangle, The EX4: Exe 5A **12**
Quadrant, The EX2: Exe 5F **5** (1B **26**)
Quarries, The EX4: Exe 2D **24**
Quarry La. EX2: Sow, Won 1F **27**
Quarry Pk. Rd. EX2: Won 2G **27**
Quarter Mile La. EX5: Mar G 6H **17**
Quay, The EX2: Exe 5D **4** (1A **26**)
Quay Hill EX2: Exe 5C **4** (1H **25**)
Quay House Vis. Cen. 5D **4** (1H **25**)
Quay La. EX2: Exe 5D **4** (1A **26**)
 EX8: Lymp 3A **42**
Quay Steps EX2: Exe 5D **4**
Queen's Ct. *EX8: Exmth* *3C **48***
 (off Queen St.)
Queen's Cres. EX4: Exe 1E **5** (5A **12**)
Queen's Dr. EX8: Exmth 4D **48**
Queens Drive, The EX4: Exe 3H **11**
Queensland Dr. EX4: Exe 2C **12**
Queen's Rd. EX2: Exe 6B **4** (3G **25**)
 EX9: Bud S 3F **45**
Queens Sq. EX5: Broadc 3E **7**
Queen's Ter. EX4: Exe 1B **4** (5H **11**)
Queen St. EX4: Exe 1C **4** (5H **11**)
 EX8: Exmth 3C **48**
 EX9: Bud S 5G **45**
 EX14: Hon 3E **23**
Queens Wlk. EX4: Exe 2C **4**
Questant La. EX10: Sidm 3E **39**
Quintet Cl. EX1: Heav 1G **27**

R

Raceworld 1H **35**
Rackclose La. EX4: Exe 4B **4** (1H **25**)
Rackfield Cotts. EX4: Exe 4F **11**
Rack St. EX1: Exe 4C **4** (1H **25**)
Raddenstile Ct. EX8: Exmth 3D **48**
Raddenstile La. EX8: Exmth 3D **48**
Radford Rd. EX2: Exe 5E **5** (1A **26**)
Radnor Pl. EX2: Exe 4F **5** (1B **26**)
Radway EX10: Sidm 5D **38**
Radway Cinema, The
 Scott Cinemas 5D **38**
Radway Pl. EX10: Sidm 5D **38**
Ragg La. EX9: Bud S 5G **45**
Rag La. EX5: Rock 6G **17**
 (not continuous)
Raglans EX2: Alph 6A **26**
Railway Cotts. EX1: Whip 6G **13**
Raleigh Ct. EX10: Sidm 2D **38**
Raleigh Ct. EX9: Bud S 3H **45**
Raleigh Ho. EX2: Exe 4G **5**
 EX10: Sidm *2D **38***
 (off Raleigh Cl.)

Raleigh Rd. EX1: Exe 3G **5** (1B **26**)
 EX8: Exmth 3C **48**
 EX9: Bud S 3H **45**
 EX11: Ott M 1E **21**
Rance Dr. EX8: Exmth 4G **43**
Randell's Grn. EX8: Exmth 3G **49**
Ransom Pickard EX4: Exe 4A **12**
RATSLOE 2A **6**
Raven Cl. EX4: Exe 3A **12**
Rayners EX6: Kennf 5A **30**
Read Cl. EX8: Exmth 6E **43**
Rectory Cl. EX5: Whim 4A **8**
Rectory Dr. EX2: Alph 6H **25**
Rectory Gdns. EX3: Clyst G 2A **34**
Redcliff Ct. EX9: Bud S 5G **45**
Red Cow Village EX4: Exe 4G **11**
Reddaway Dr. EX6: Exmin 3H **31**
REDHILLS 6E **11**
Redhills EX4: Exe 5D **10**
 EX9: Bud S 5G **45**
Redhills Cl. EX4: Exe 6E **11**
Redlands, The EX10: Sidm 6C **38**
Redlands Cl. EX4: Whip 4E **13**
Red Lion La. EX1: Exe 1F **5** (5B **12**)
Redvers Rd. EX4: Exe 1G **25**
Redwood Cl. EX8: Exmth 4F **43**
 EX14: Hon 5B **22**
Redwood Rd. EX10: Sidm 4D **38**
Regatta Ct. EX8: Exmth 3A **48**
Regency Cres. EX8: Exmth 3E **49**
Regency Ga. EX10: Sidm 4E **39**
Regents Ga. EX8: Exmth 3D **48**
Regent's Pk. EX1: Heav 6C **12**
 (not continuous)
Regent Sq. EX1: Heav 1D **26**
Regent St. EX2: Exe 3G **25**
Reme Dr. EX14: Hon 5B **22**
Rennes Dr. EX4: Exe 3A **12**
Rennes Ho. EX1: Whip 5F **13**
Renslade Ho. EX4: Exe 5B **4**
Resolution Rd. EX2: Cou W 5H **27**
Retail Pk. Cl. EX2: Mar B 3H **25**
Retreat, The EX8: Exmth 2F **49**
Retreat Drive, The EX3: Top 2D **32**
Retreat Rd. EX3: Top 2E **33**
Rewe La. EX5: Rock, Whim 2G **17**
Rews Mdw. EX1: Pin 3B **14**
Rews Pk. Dr. EX1: Pin 3B **14**
Rexona Cl. EX2: Exe 4G **25**
Reynolds Cl. EX4: Pin 3H **13**
Rhode Island Dr. EX2: Cou W 5A **28**
Ribston Av. EX1: Heav 6G **13**
Ribston Cl. EX1: Heav 6G **13**
Rices M. EX2: Exe 2G **25**
Richards Cl. EX8: Exmth 5F **43**
Richmond Ct. EX4: Exe 2B **4** (6H **11**)
Richmond Rd. EX4: Exe 2B **4** (6H **11**)
 EX8: Exmth 2F **49**
Ridge Way EX6: Kenton 2B **46**
Ridgeway EX4: Exe 1G **11**
 EX11: Ott M 1E **21**
 EX14: Hon 5D **22**
Ridgeway Ct. EX2: Cou W 1H **5** (5C **12**)
Ridgeway Gdns. EX11: Ott M 1E **21**
Ridgeway Mead EX10: Sidm 2B **38**
Ridings, The EX3: Ebf 4A **34**
Rifford Rd. EX2: Won 2E **27**
Ringswell Av. EX1: Heav 6G **13**
Ringswell Pk. EX2: Won 1G **27**
Ripon Cl. EX1: Exe 6E **11**
River Front EX3: Exton 6H **33**
Rivermead Av. EX8: Exmth 5C **42**
Rivermead Ct. EX8: Exmth 4C **42**
Rivermead Rd. EX2: Exe 3B **26**
River Plate Rd. EX2: Cou W 5H **27**
Riverside *EX10: Sidm* *5D **38***
 (off York St.)

Riverside Cl. EX14: Hon 3D 22
Riverside Ct. EX2: Exe 5D 4
Riverside Leisure Cen. 6B 4 (2H 25)
Riverside Rd. EX3: Top 2E 33
EX10: Sidm 5D 38
Riverside Ter. EX10: Sidm 5D 38
(off York St.)
Riverside Valley Pk. 4B 26
Riverside Vw. EX11: Ott M 2D 20
Riversmeet EX3: Top 5G 33
Rivers Wlk. EX2: Cou W 1C 32
Riverview Dr. EX4: Exe 4F 11
River Vw. Ter. EX6: Exmin 5B 32
Riviera Ter. EX6: Exmin 5B 32
Robert Davy Rd. EX2: Cou W 5H 27
Roberts Rd. EX2: Exe 5E 5 (1A 26)
Robert Way EX10: New P 1D 36
Roche Gdn. EX2: Cou W 6E 27
ROCKBEARE 2E 17
Rockbeare Hill EX5: Rock 5B 18
Rockfield Ho. EX4: Exe 1E 5
Rockside EX4: Exe 3A 4 (6G 11)
Rockside Vs. EX4: Exe 2A 4 (6G 11)
Rodney Cl. EX8: L'ham 6A 44
Rolle, The EX9: Bud S 5G 45
Rolle Barton EX9: Ott'n 4F 41
Rolle Cotts. EX9: E Bud 6D 40
EX9: Know 3D 44
Rolle Rd. EX8: Exmth 3C 48
EX9: Bud S 5G 45
Rollestone Cres. EX4: Exe 2C 12
Rolle St. EX8: Exmth 3C 48
Rolle Studios EX8: Exmth 3C 48
(off Rolle St.)
Rolle Vs. EX8: Exmth 3C 48
Roly Poly Hill EX2: Exe 4E 25
Roman Wlk. EX1: Exe 3E 5
Roman Way EX5: Cranb 3A 16
EX14: Hon 2F 23
Romsey Dr. EX2: Exe 5H 5 (1C 26)
Rookswood La. EX5: Rock 3E 17
Rookwood Cl. EX14: Hon 3D 22
Ropers Ct. EX9: Ott'n 4G 41
Roper's La. EX9: Ott'n 4G 41
Ropewalk Ho. EX8: Exmth 3A 48
(off Shelly Rd.)
Rosebank Cres. EX4: Exe 3B 12
Rosebarn Av. EX4: Exe 3B 12
Rosebarn La. EX4: Exe 2B 12
Rosebery Rd. EX4: Exe 4C 12
EX8: Exmth 1C 48
Roseland Av. EX1: Heav 6E 13
Roseland Cres. EX1: Heav 6E 13
Roseland Dr. EX1: Heav 1E 27
Roselands EX10: Sidm 5C 38
Rosemary St. EX4: Exe 1F 25
Rosemont Cl. EX2: Alph 5H 25
Rosemount Cl. EX14: Hon 4D 22
Rosemount La. EX14: Hon 4C 22
Rosemullion, The EX9: Bud S 5G 45
Rosemullion Ct. EX9: Bud S 5G 45
Roseway EX8: Exmth 1H 49
Rosewell Cl. EX14: Hon 2F 23
Rosewood Cres. EX5: Clyst M 4G 29
Rosewood Ter. EX4: Exe 4B 12
Ross Cl. EX1: Pin 3B 14
Roswell Cl. EX8: Exmth 4D 48
Rougemont Ct. EX6: Exmin 4H 31
Roundball Cl. EX14: Hon 5E 23
Roundball La. EX14: Hon 6D 22
Roundhill Cl. EX4: Exe 1G 11
Roundhouse La. EX8: Exmth 5D 42
Roundtable Meet EX4: Whip 3F 13
Rowan Cl. EX14: Hon 5B 22
Rowancroft EX1: Heav 6D 12
Rowan Way EX4: Exe 5F 11
Rowcroft Cl. EX14: Hon 4D 22

Rowe Ho. EX4: Exe 4A 12
Rowhorne Rd. EX4: Nad 2A 10
Rowlstone Cl. EX8: Exmth 4E 43
Royal Albert Memorial Museum &
Art Gallery 2C 4 (6H 11)
Royal Av. EX8: Exmth 2B 48
Royal Cl. EX2: Alph 1D 30
Royal Cres. EX2: Sow 3H 27
ROYAL DEVON & EXETER HOSPITAL
Heavitree 3H 5 (6C 12)
Wonford 1D 26
Royal Way EX6: Star 1F 47
Royston Ct. EX1: Whip 4G 13
Rugby Rd. EX4: Exe 6A 4 (2G 25)
Rushforth Pl. EX4: Exe 4E 11
Russell Cl. EX9: E Bud 5D 40
Russell Dr. EX9: E Bud 5D 40
Russell St. EX1: Exe 2F 5 (6B 12)
EX10: Sidm 6D 38
Russell Ter. EX4: Exe 1B 4
(off Little Silver)
Russell Wlk. EX2: Sow 3G 27
Russell Way EX2: Cou W, Sow 3G 27
Russet Av. EX1: Heav 6G 13
Russet Cl. EX1: Heav 6G 13
Rutherford St. EX2: Won 2E 27
Rydal M. EX4: Exe 1F 25
(off Windermere Cl.)
Rydon La. EX2: Cou W, Sow 5F 27
EX3: Exton 6B 34
EX5: Wood 6B 34
EX9: Ott'n 3G 41
Rydon La. Retail Pk.
EX2: Sow 3G 27
Rydon Pk. EX2: Sow 2H 27
Ryll Cl. EX8: Exmth 2D 48
Ryll Ct. Dr. EX8: Exmth 2D 48
Ryll Gro. EX8: Exmth 2D 48
Ryll La. EX9: Bud S 5H 45

Saddlers La. EX11: Ott M 2D 20
Sadler Cl. EX8: Exmth 1G 49
Sages Lea EX5: Wood S 2G 35
Sailmakers Ct. EX8: Exmth 3A 48
St Albans Cl. EX4: Exe 6E 11
St Andrew's Cl. EX14: Fen 1H 9
St Andrews Ho. EX8: Exmth 3B 48
(off St Andrew's Rd.)
St Andrew's Rd. EX4: Exe 1F 11
EX5: Cow 1E 11
EX8: Exmth 3B 48
St Annes EX6: Kenton 1A 46
St Anne's Chapel EX4: Exe 1G 5
St Annes Rd. EX1: Heav 5C 12
St Anthony's Cl. EX11: Ott M 1E 21
St Bernard's Cl. EX2: Exe 2B 26
St Briac Way EX8: Exmth 4G 43
St Budeaux Cl. EX11: Ott M 2E 21
St Budeaux Orchard EX11: Ott M 2E 21
St Catherine's Chapel & Almshouse (ruins)
. . . . .3D 4
(off Bedford St.)
St Clements La. EX4: Exe 1A 4 (5H 11)
St Cyres Rd. EX14: Hon 3D 22
ST DAVID'S 5G 11
St David's Hill EX4: Exe 1A 4 (5G 11)
St Davids Pl. EX4: Exe 5G 11
(off Red Cow Village)
St Davids Ter. EX4: Exe 2B 4 (6H 11)
St Edmonds Ct. EX4: Exe 4B 4
St George's Ter. EX2: Shil G 4A 30
St German's EX4: Exe 4A 12
St German's Rd. EX4: Exe 4A 12
St Helens Rd. EX10: Sidm 6B 38

St Hilarian EX8: Exmth 4D 48
St Hill Cl. EX2: Exe 4G 25
St Ida's Cl. EX2: Ide 5D 24
ST JAMES' .4B 12
St James Cl. EX4: Exe 5B 12
St James' Park Station (Rail) 5B 12
St James' Rd. EX4: Exe 5B 12
St James Ter. EX4: Exe 5B 12
St John Cl. EX14: Hon 3E 23
St John's Farm M.
EX8: Exmth 4H 43
St Johns Pl. EX1: Exe 3D 4
St John's Rd. EX1: Heav 1H 5 (5C 12)
EX8: Exmth 6F 43
(not continuous)
St Johns Vs. EX2: Heav 1D 26
St Katherine's Rd. EX4: Whip 4E 13
St Lawrence Cres. EX1: Heav 6H 13
ST LEONARD'S 5H 5 (1C 26)
St Leonard's Av.
EX2: Exe 6E 5 (2A 26)
St Leonards Pl. EX2: Exe 5F 5 (1B 26)
EX5: Clyst M 3C 28
St Leonards Rd. EX2: Exe . . .6F 5 (2B 26)
EX14: Hon 4C 22
ST LOYE'S .2E 27
St Loyes Gdns. EX2: Won 1F 27
St Loyes Rd. EX2: Won 1E 27
St Loyes Ter. EX2: Won 2E 27
St Luke's Sports Cen. 3H 5 (6C 12)
St Lukes Vw. EX2: Cou W 5D 26
St Malo Cl. EX8: Exmth 4G 43
St Margarets Ter. EX3: Top 3F 33
(off Exe St.)
St Margaret's Vw. EX8: L'ham 6A 44
St Marks Av. EX1: Heav 5D 12
St Mark's Rd. EX14: Hon 5C 22
St Martins Cl. EX10: Sidm 2D 38
St Martins Ct. EX10: Sidm 3D 38
(off St Martins Cl.)
St Mary's Arches EX4: Exe . . .3C 4 (6H 11)
St Marys Pk. EX11: Ott M 2E 21
St Mary Steps Ter. EX1: Exe 4C 4
St Marys Vw. EX11: W Hill 4G 19
St Matthews Cl. EX1: Exe 2G 5 (6B 12)
St Matthews Ct. EX1: Exe 2G 5
St Matthews Wlk.
EX1: Exe 2G 5 (6B 12)
St Michaels Cl. EX2: Alph 5H 25
EX5: Clyst H 4F 15
EX9: Ott'n 4G 41
St Michaels Hill EX5: Clyst H 4F 15
St Michael's M. EX4: Exe 2B 4
St Michaels Way EX5: Cranb 2B 16
St Nicholas Priory 4B 4
St Olaves Cl. EX4: Exe 4C 4 (6H 11)
St Olaves M. EX4: Exe 3B 4
St Pauls Cl. EX2: Won 3D 26
St Paul's Rd. EX14: Hon 5C 22
St Peters Ct. EX10: Sidm 6D 38
(off Church St.)
St Peters Ho. EX2: Exe 5D 4
St Peters Mt. EX2: Exe 5D 10
St Peter's Rd. EX14: Hon 4C 22
St Petrock's Cl. EX2: Exe 5G 5 (1B 26)
St Saviours Rd. EX11: Ott M 2D 20
St Sevan Way EX8: Exmth 4G 43
St Sidwell's Av. EX4: Exe 1F 5 (5A 12)
ST THOMAS 6A 4 (2G 25)
St Thomas Ct. EX4: Exe 6A 4 (2G 25)
St Thomas M. EX2: Exe 2G 25
St Thomas Shop. Cen.
EX4: Exe 5A 4 (2G 25)
St Thomas Station (Rail) 6A 4 (2G 25)
Salcombe Cl. EX10: Sidm 5E 39
Salcombe Hill EX10: Sidm 5E 39
Salcombe Hill Cl. EX10: Sidm 5D 38

Salcombe Hill Rd. EX10: Sidm 5D 38
Salcombe Lawn EX10: Sidm 5D 38
SALCOMBE REGIS 3H 39
Salcombe Regis Camping & Caravan Pk.
  EX10: Sal R 2H 39
Salcombe Rd. EX10: Sidm 5D 38
Salem Chapel 4D 40
Salem Pl. EX4: Exe 1G 5 (5B 12)
Salisbury Av. EX14: Fen 1H 9
Salisbury Cl. EX14: Fen 1H 9
Salisbury Rd. EX4: Exe 4C 12
  EX8: Exmth 2C 48
Salmon Pool La. EX2: Exe 3C 26
Salston Barton EX11: Ott M 3C 20
Salston Ride EX11: Ott M 3B 20
Salterne Mdws. EX9: Bud S 3G 45
Salter's Ct. EX2: Won 2E 27
Salters Mdw. EX10: Sidm 4D 38
Salter's Rd. EX2: Won 2E 27
Salterton Ct. EX8: Exmth 1H 49
Salterton Rd. EX8: Exmth 3D 48
  EX9: Know 3D 48
Salting Hill EX9: Bud S 5H 45
Salutary Mt. EX1: Heav 1D 26
Sampson Cl. EX10: Sidm 1C 38
Sampson's Hill EX2: Shil G 4B 30
Sampsons La. EX1: Heav 1H 5 (5C 12)
Sanderling Ct. EX2: Sow 6B 14
Sanders Cl. EX5: Broadc 4F 7
Sanders Rd. EX4: Pin 3H 13
Sandfords EX6: Kennf 5B 30
Sandford Wlk. EX1: Exe 2G 5 (6B 12)
  (not continuous)
Sandgate La. EX11: Wigg 5C 20
Sandhill St. EX11: Ott M 1D 20
Sandpiper Ct. EX4: Pin 3H 13
Sandpiper Dr. EX3: Exton 6A 34
Sandpiper Grn. EX2: Exe 2D 24
SANDYGATE 4B 28
Sandy La. EX4: Polt 1A 6
  EX5: Broadc 5F 7
Sandy Park Stadium 4A 28
Sandy Pk. Way EX2: Cou W 3A 28
Sanford Pl. EX2: Exe 2G 25
Sannerville Way EX6: Exmin 2A 32
Sargent Cl. EX1: Heav 6G 13
Sarlsdown Rd. EX8: Exmth 2F 49
Savile Rd. EX4: Exe 1F 25
Savoy Cinema, The
  Scott Cinemas 3C 48
  (off Rolle St.)
Savoy Hill EX4: Whip 2E 13
Sawmill La. EX9: E Bud 4B 40
Sawmills Way EX14: Hon 4E 23
Saxon Av. EX4: Pin 2A 14
Saxon Rd. EX1: Heav 6D 12
Scarsdale EX8: Exmth 4E 49
School Hill EX5: Whim 4A 8
  EX6: Cockw 3F 47
  EX8: Lymp 2A 42
School La. EX2: Cou W 5E 27
  EX5: Broadc 3E 7
  EX8: Exmth 6D 42
  EX10: New P 1D 36
  EX11: W Hill 4F 19
  EX14: Hon 4D 23
School Rd. EX2: Exe 6A 4 (2G 25)
School St. EX10: Sidf 1E 39
Schooner's Ct. EX8: Exmth 3A 48
Scott Av. EX2: Won 3D 26
Scott Cinemas
  The Radway Cinema 5D 38
  The Savoy Cinema 3C 48
  (off Rolle St.)
Scott Dr. EX8: Exmth 5D 42
Scratch Face La. EX2: Ide 4B 24
Seabrook Av. EX2: Cou W 1C 32

Seabrook M. EX2: Cou W 1C 32
Seafield Av. EX8: Exmth 5C 42
Seafield La. EX10: Sidm 6C 38
Seafield Rd. EX10: Sidm 5C 38
Seasons, The EX4: Whip 4G 13
  (off Summerway)
Sea Vw. Ter. EX10: Sidm 4C 38
Second Av. EX1: Heav 6D 12
  EX2: Cou W 1C 32
Sedemuda Cl. EX10: Sidm 1C 38
Sedemuda Rd. EX10: Sidm 1B 38
Sedgeclaire Cl. EX1: Pin 3B 14
Senate Ct. EX8: Exmth 6G 43
  (off Senate Way)
Senate Way EX8: Exmth 6F 43
Sentrys Orchard EX6: Exmin 5B 32
Sercombes Gdns. EX6: Star 1F 47
Serge Ct. EX2: Exe 5C 4
Seven Acres EX5: Cranb 3A 16
Seven Stones La. EX10: Sidm 5H 37
Seymour Ct. EX8: Exmth 5D 42
Seymour Rd. EX8: Exmth 5D 42
Shackleton Cl. EX8: Exmth 5D 42
Shaftesbury Rd. EX2: Exe 2G 25
Shakespeare Rd. EX2: Won 3D 26
Shakespeare Way EX8: Exmth 3E 43
Shapter Ct. EX8: L'ham 2H 49
Sharps Ct. EX8: Exmth 3A 48
Shauls Ct. EX1: Exe 1F 5
Shearman Ct. EX2: Exe 5C 4 (1H 25)
Sheirs Orchard EX9: Yett 3A 40
Shelley Cl. EX2: Exe 4G 25
Shelly Ct. EX8: Exmth 3A 48
Shelly Reach EX8: Exmth 3B 48
Shelly Rd. EX8: Exmth 3A 48
Shelton Pl. EX1: Heav 6D 12
Shepherds Hill EX2: Cou W 5E 27
  (off Countess Wear Rd.)
Shepherds La. EX10: Col R 4C 36
Sheppard Rd. EX4: Exe 2B 12
Sheppards Row EX8: Exmth 2C 48
Sherbrook Cl. EX9: Bud S 5F 45
Sherbrook Hill EX9: Bud S 5F 45
Shercroft Cl. EX5: Broadc 2G 15
Sheridan Rd. EX4: Whip 4G 13
Sherwells Cl. EX7: Daw W 6E 47
Sherwood Cl. EX2: Won 1D 26
Sherwood Dr. EX8: Exmth 4F 43
SHILLINGFORD ABBOT 2C 30
Shillingford La. EX6: Kennf 4C 30
Shillingford Rd.
  EX2: Alph, Shil A 1C 30
SHILLINGFORD ST GEORGE 4A 30
Ship La. EX5: Clyst H 4F 15
Shipley Rd. EX14: Hon 3F 23
Shirehampton Ho. EX4: Exe 2A 4
Shirley Cl. EX8: Exmth 3F 43
Shooting Marsh Stile
  EX2: Exe 6B 4 (2H 25)
Shortridge Cl. EX4: Hon 5E 23
Shortwood Cl. EX9: Bud S 3F 45
Shortwood La. EX9: Know 6A 40
Shrubbery, The EX4: Exe 3D 12
Shute Mdw. St. EX8: Exmth 2C 48
  (off Meadow St.)
Shutes Mead EX11: Ott M 1E 21
Shutterton La.
  EX7: Daw, Daw W 6D 46
SID 4E 39
Sidcliffe EX10: Sidm 3E 39
SIDFORD 1E 39
Sidford High St.
  EX10: Sidf, Stow 1B 38
Sidford Rd. EX10: Sidm 3D 38
Sidgard Rd. EX10: Sidm 3E 39
Sidlands EX10: Sidm 5C 38
Sid La. EX10: Sidm 3D 38

Sidleigh EX10: Sidm 4E 39
Sidmount Gdns. EX10: Sidm 4C 38
SIDMOUTH 6D 38
Sidmouth Golf Course 6A 38
Sidmouth Mus. 6D 38
Sidmouth Rd. EX2: Sow 3B 28
  EX2: Sow, Won 1G 27
  EX5: Clyst M 4D 28
  EX11: Ott M, Wigg 2E 21
  EX14: Hon 5C 22
Sidmouth Sports Cen. 2E 39
Sidmouth Swimming Pool 6D 38
SIDMOUTH VICTORIA HOSPITAL .5C 38
Sid Pk. Rd. EX10: Sidm 4D 38
Sid Rd. EX10: Sidm 5D 38
Sid Vale Cl. EX10: Sidf 1F 39
Sid Vale M. EX10: Sidf 1E 39
  (off Sid Vale Cl.)
Sidwell Ho. EX1: Exe 2E 5
Sidwell St. EX4: Exe 2E 5 (6A 12)
Sigford Rd. EX2: Mar B 6B 26
Signals, The EX14: Fen 1H 9
Silver Birch Cl. EX2: Won 3E 27
Silverdale EX8: Exmth 4G 43
Silverdown Office Pk.
  EX5: Clyst H 6B 16
Silver La. EX4: Exe 1G 5 (5B 12)
  EX5: Rock 3E 17
Silverlea Cotts. EX5: Tala 1E 9
Silvers, The EX3: Top 4B 28
Silver St. EX11: Ott M 1D 20
  EX14: Hon 3E 23
Silver Ter. EX4: Exe 2B 4 (6H 11)
Silverton Rd. EX2: Mar B 6B 26
Simey Cl. EX4: Exe 5F 11
Sir Alex Wlk. EX3: Top 2D 32
Sir Christopher Ondaatje
  Indoor Cricket Centre, The 3H 11
Sivell Ct. EX2: Heav 1D 26
  (off Sivell Pl.)
Sivell M. EX2: Heav 1D 26
  (off Sivell Pl.)
Sivell Pl. EX2: Heav 1D 26
Skinners Cl. EX10: Sidm 5B 38
Skyways Bus. Pk. EX5: Clyst H ...6B 16
Slade Cl. EX11: Ott M 1F 21
Slade Rd. EX11: Ott M 2F 21
Sleap Hill EX9: E Bud 4E 41
Sleepy Hollow EX2: Cou W 1C 32
  (off Moon Ridge)
Slewton Cres. EX5: Whim 3A 8
Slittercombe La. EX6: Kenton 1B 46
Small La. EX5: Broadc 3E 7
Smith Fld. Rd. EX2: Alph 6G 25
Smiths Ct. EX2: Exe 2H 25
Smythen St. EX1: Exe 4C 4 (1H 25)
Snowdrop Cl. EX14: Hon 5C 22
Snowdrop M. EX4: Exe 4D 10
Solar Cres. EX4: Exe 2F 25
Somerset Av. EX4: Exe 2E 25
Somerville Cl. EX8: Exmth 6F 43
South Av. EX1: Heav 2H 5 (6C 12)
Southbrook La. EX5: Whim 1E 17
Southbrook Rd. EX2: Cou W 4E 27
Southernhay E. EX1: Exe 4D 4 (1A 26)
  (not continuous)
Southernhay Gdns.
  EX1: Exe 3E 5 (6A 12)
  (not continuous)
Southernhay W. EX1: Exe 4E 5 (1A 26)
  (not continuous)
Southern Rd. EX8: Exmth 1C 48
Southern Wood EX8: Exmth 5G 43
Sth. Farm Rd. EX9: Bud S 3H 45
Southgate EX2: Exe 5D 4 (1A 26)
Southgate Ct. EX2: Exe 5D 4
  (off Holloway St.)

South Grange EX2: Sow 3H 27
Sth. Hayes Mdw. EX5: Cranb 3A 16
Southlands EX1: Heav 6C 12
South Lawn EX2: Exe 4F 5
  EX10: Sidm 1E 39
Sth. Lawn Ter. EX1: Heav 6D 12
South Pde. EX9: Bud S 5H 45
Southport Av. EX4: Exe 1E 25
South St. EX1: Exe 3C 4 (6H 11)
  EX8: Exmth 3C 48
South Ter. EX8: Lymp 2B 42
SOUTH TOWN 2C 46
South Town EX6: Kenton 1C 46
South Vw. Pasture
  EX5: Cranb 3A 16
South Vw. Ter. EX4: Exe 4B 12
  EX6: Exmin 4B 32
Southway EX10: Sidm 5E 39
Sovereign Cl. EX8: Exmth 6G 43
Sovereign Ct. EX2: Sow 3H 27
Sowden La. EX8: Lymp 3A 42
SOWTON 6D 14
Sowton (Park & Ride) 2A 28
Sowton Ind. Est. EX2: Sow 1A 28
  (not continuous)
Sowton La. EX5: Sow 5C 14
Spacex .4C 4
Spencer Cl. EX8: Exmth 5G 43
Spencer Ct. EX11: Ott M 2D 20
  (off St Saviours Rd.)
Spenser Av. EX2: Won 3D 26
Spicer Rd. EX1: Exe 4F 5 (1B 26)
Spider's La. EX8: Exmth 4E 43
Spindlewood Cl. EX14: Hon 6E 23
Spinnakers EX8: Exmth 3A 48
  (off Shelly Rd.)
Spinney Cl. EX2: Won 2G 27
Spinning Path EX4: Exe 5B 12
  (off Black Boy Rd.)
Spitup La. EX10: Sidm 2A 38
Springfield Rd. EX4: Exe 4B 12
  EX8: Exmth 6D 42
  EX14: Hon 4G 23
Spring Gdns. EX11: Ott M 2E 21
Spruce Cl. EX4: Whip 2F 13
  EX8: Exmth 4F 43
Spurway Hill EX6: Exmin 5H 31
Square, The EX4: Exe 4F 11
  EX5: Rock 3E 17
  EX5: Whim 4A 8
  EX10: Sidm 2B 38
Staddon Cl. EX4: Exe 5F 13
Stadium Way EX4: Exe 5B 12
Stadway Mdw. EX10: Sidm 4A 38
Staffick Cl. EX6: Kenton 1B 46
Stafford Rd. EX4: Exe 1F 25
Stanford Rd. EX2: Won 1G 27
Stanhope Dr. EX10: Sidm 3D 38
Stanley M. EX9: Bud S 4G 45
Stanley Sq. EX3: Top 4F 33
Stanley Wlk. EX8: Exmth 3F 43
Stantyway Rd. EX9: Ott'n 6H 41
Stanwey EX1: Heav 1E 27
Staplake La. EX6: Star 2D 46
Staplake Rd. EX6: Star 1F 47
Staple's Bldgs. EX8: Exmth 2C 48
  (off Crudges La.)
Staples M. EX8: Exmth 2C 48
  (off Exeter Rd.)
Star Barton La. EX5: Cow 1B 10
STARCROSS 1F 47
Starcross Fishing & Cruising Club . .1F 47
Starcross Station (Rail) 1F 47
Station Rd. EX1: Pin 3A 14
  EX2: Ide 5C 24
  EX3: Exton 6A 34
  EX3: Top 3F 33

Station Rd. EX4: Exe 4F 11
  EX5: Broadc 5F 7
  EX6: Exmin 5C 32
  EX9: Bud S 4G 45
  EX10: Harp, New P 1D 36
  EX10: Sidm 4C 38
  EX14: Fen 1H 9
Station Yd. EX4: Exe 1B 4 (5H 11)
  EX10: Sidm 3C 38
  EX14: Hon 4E 23
Steel Cl. EX14: Hon 3F 23
Steeple Dr. EX2: Alph 1D 30
Stepcote Hill EX1: Exe 4C 4 (1H 25)
Stephen St. EX4: Exe 3D 4 (6A 12)
Steps Cl. EX1: Pin 3B 14
Steven's Cross EX10: Sidf 1F 39
Steven's Cross Cl. EX10: Sidf 1G 39
Stevens La. EX10: Sidm 2C 38
Stevenstone Rd. EX8: Exmth 2F 49
Stewart Cl. EX8: Exmth 6G 43
Stintway La. EX10: Sidm 5A 38
Stocker Rd. EX4: Exe 3H 11
STOKE HILL 3C 12
Stoke Hill EX4: Exe 3C 12
Stoke Hill Cres. EX4: Exe 3C 12
Stoke Lyne EX8: Exmth 6E 43
Stoke Mdw. Cl. EX4: Exe 2C 12
Stoke Rd. EX4: Exe 1F 11
Stokes Mead EX5: Wood 5G 35
Stoke Valley Rd. EX4: Exe 1A 12
Stoneborough Ct. EX9: Bud S 4H 45
Stoneborough La. EX9: Bud S 4H 45
Stone Cl. EX14: Hon 5D 22
Stone La. EX2: Exe 3G 25
  EX8: Lymp 2A 42
Stone La. Retail Pk. EX2: Mar B 3H 25
Stoneyford Pk. EX9: Bud S 4H 45
Stoneylands EX5: Rock 3D 16
Stoney La. EX14: Hon 6E 23
Stony La. EX5: Wood S 2G 35
Stover Ct. EX1: Exe 1F 5 (5B 12)
Stowbrook EX10: Sidm 1B 38
STOWFORD
  EX10, Higher Woolbrook 1A 38
  EX10, Yettington 1C 40
Stowford Ri. EX10: Sidm 2B 38
Strand EX3: Top 4F 33
  EX8: Exmth 3C 48
Strand, The EX6: Star 1F 47
  EX8: Lymp 2A 42
Strand Ct. EX3: Top 4F 33
Strand Vw. EX3: Top 4F 33
Stratford Av. EX4: Whip 4G 13
Strawberry Av. EX2: Alph 6A 26
Strawberry Hill EX8: Lymp 2A 42
Strawberry La. EX11: Ott M 3B 20
Stream Ct. EX2: Exe 6C 4 (2H 25)
Streamers Mdws. EX14: Hon 4E 23
Streatham Dr. EX4: Exe 4G 11
Streatham Ri. EX4: Exe 4G 11
Streatham Sports Pk. 3H 11
STRETE RALEGH 1C 18
Stuart Rd. EX1: Heav 6D 12
Sturges Rd. EX8: Exmth 1F 49
Sullivan Rd. EX2: Won 1G 27
Summer Cl. EX4: Whip 4F 13
  EX8: Exmth 1G 49
Summerfield EX5: Wood 4G 35
  EX10: Sidm 1D 38
Summerland EX14: Hon 4E 23
Summerland Ga. EX1: Exe 2F 5
Summerland St. EX1: Exe 1F 5 (5B 12)
Summer La. EX4: Whip 3F 13
  EX8: Exmth 4C 42
Summer Mdw. EX5: Cranb 2A 16
Summerway EX4: Whip 4F 13
Sunhill Av. EX3: Top 2F 33

Sunhill La. EX3: Top 2F 33
Sunnybank EX6: Kenton 1B 46
Sunnyfield EX5: Broadc 3E 7
Sunnyhill EX11: Ott M 1E 21
Sunnymoor Cl. EX1: Pin 3B 14
Sunnyside EX10: New P 1D 36
  EX14: Awli 2A 22
Sunwine Pl. EX8: Exmth 3D 48
Surbiton Cres. EX4: Exe 2F 25
Sussex Cl. EX4: Exe 2E 25
Sutherlake Gdns. EX5: Broadc 4G 7
Swains Ct. EX3: Top 3E 33
Swains Rd. EX9: Bud S 3H 45
Swallow Ct. EX2: Exe 4F 11
Swallow Dr. EX2: Exe 3D 24
Swallowfield Rd. EX2: Cou W 4E 27
Swan Ct. EX2: Exe 6F 5 (2B 26)
Swan Rd. EX6: Star 2E 47
Swan Units EX2: Sow 1A 28
Swan Yd. EX4: Exe 5A 4 (1G 25)
Sweetbrier La. EX1: Heav 6E 13
Swiss Cl. EX8: Exmth 4D 42
Sycamore Cl. EX1: Heav 1F 27
  EX5: Broadc 4F 7
  EX8: Exmth 5G 43
  EX14: Hon 5C 22
Sydenham Ho. EX1: Exe 1H 5
Sydney Pl. EX2: Exe 6B 4
Sydney Rd. EX2: Exe 2G 25
Sylvan Av. EX4: Exe 3B 12
Sylvan Cl. EX8: Exmth 5C 42
Sylvan Ct. EX8: Exmth 5C 42
  (off Exeter Rd.)
Sylvania Dr. EX4: Exe 2C 12
Sylvan Rd. EX4: Exe 3B 12
Synagogue Pl. EX4: Exe 3C 4 (6H 11)

T

Tabernacle Ct. EX1: Exe 5C 4
Taddiforde Rd. EX4: Exe 5G 11
Taddyforde Ct. EX4: Exe 4G 11
  (off Taddyforde Est.)
Taddyforde Ct. Mans. EX4: Exe 4G 11
  (off Taddyforde Est.)
Taddyforde Est. EX4: Exe 4G 11
Talaton Rd. EX5: Whim 4B 8
Tamarisk Cl. EX4: Whip 2F 13
Tan La. EX2: Exe 3H 25
Tape La. EX14: Awli 3A 22
Tappers Cl. EX3: Top 3F 33
Taps Cl. EX6: Exmin 4B 32
Tarbet Av. EX1: Heav 5D 12
Taunton Cl. EX2: Exe 3G 25
Tavistock Rd. EX4: Exe 1A 4 (5G 11)
Taylor Cl. EX11: Ott M 1B 20
Teazle Ct. EX2: Exe 5C 4
Tedburn Rd. EX4: Exe, White 6A 10
Tedstone La. EX8: Lymp 1C 42
Telegraph La. EX5: Rock 3D 18
Telford Rd. EX4: Exe 1A 4 (5G 11)
Temple Gdns. EX10: Sidm 4D 38
Temple Rd. EX2: Exe 5E 5 (1A 26)
Temple St. EX10: Sidm 4D 38
Tennyson Av. EX2: Won 3D 26
Tennyson Way EX8: Exmth 3E 43
Terracina Ct. EX2: Exe 6D 4
Thackeray Rd. EX4: Whip 4G 13
The . . . .
  Names prefixed with 'The' for example
  'The Arch' are indexed under the
  main name such as 'Arch, The'
Thelma Hulbert Gallery, The 3E 23
Third Av. EX1: Heav 6D 12
  EX2: Cou W 1C 32
  EX2: Won 1H 27

Thomas Cl. EX8: Exmth 3E **43**
Thomas La. *EX4: Exe* 4G **11**
(off Harefield Cl.)
Thompson Rd. EX1: Heav 5E **13**
Thornberry Av. EX1: Whip 6F **13**
Thorn Cl. EX1: Whip 6F **13**
Thorndale Courts EX4: Exe 4D **10**
Thorne Farm Way
EX11: Ott M 1C **20**
Thornfield Cl. EX8: Exmth 5C **42**
Thorn Park Golf Cen. 2H **39**
Thornton Cl. EX9: Bud S 5G **45**
Thornton Hill EX4: Exe 4A **12**
Thorntree Bus. Units
EX8: Exmth 6H **43**
Thorpe Av. EX8: Exmth 4D **42**
Thorverton Rd. EX2: Mar B 6B **26**
Three Corner Fld.
EX5: Cranb 3A **16**
Three Corner Pl. EX2: Alph 6A **26**
Thurlow Rd. EX4: Exe 4C **12**
Thursby Wlk. EX4: Pin 3H **13**
Tidwell Cl. EX9: Bud S 3G **45**
Tidwell La. EX9: E Bud 1G **45**
Tidwell Rd. EX9: Bud S 3G **45**
Tin La. EX2: Exe 6A **4** (2G **25**)
Tintagel Cl. EX4: Whip 2E **13**
Tip Hill EX11: Ott M 2D **20**
Tipton La. EX11: W Hill 2G **19**
Tithebarn Copse EX1: Pin 4B **14**
Tithebarn La. EX1: Pin 4B **14**
Toadpit La. EX11: W Hill 3G **19**
Toby La. EX5: Wood S 3H **35**
Tollards Rd. EX2: Cou W 5E **27**
TOPSHAM .3F **33**
Topsham Mus. 4F **33**
Topsham Pool 3F **33**
Topsham Rd.
EX2: Cou W, Exe 6E **5** (2B **26**)
Topsham Station (Rail) 3F **33**
Tor Cl. EX4: Whip 3E **13**
Toronto Ho. EX4: Exe 4C **12**
Toronto Rd. EX4: Exe 5B **12**
Torrington Pl. *EX6: Kenton* 1A **46**
(off Chiverstone Rd.)
Tottons Ct. EX2: Alph 6G **25**
Tourist Info. Cen.
Budleigh Salterton 5G **45**
Exeter 2E **5** (6A **12**)
Exmouth 3C **48**
Honiton .3E **23**
Ottery St Mary 2D **20**
Sidmouth 6D **38**
Tovey M. *EX14: Hon* 3E **23**
(off King St.)
Towerfield EX3: Top 1E **33**
Tower Rd. EX14: Hon 6H **23**
Tower St. EX8: Exmth 3C **48**
Tower Vw. EX5: Broadc 5E **7**
Tower Wlk. EX2: Alph 6A **26**
Town End EX5: Broadc 3F **7**
Town Farm Cl. EX14: Hon 3D **22**
Townfield EX6: Exmin 4A **32**
Town Hill EX5: Broadc 3E **7**
Town La. EX5: Wood 5G **35**
Towsington La. EX6: Exmin 6H **31**
Tracey Vw. *EX14: Hon* 3D **22**
(off Northcote La.)
Trafalgar Ct. *EX3: Top* 1E **33**
(off High St.)
Trafalgar Pl. EX4: Exe 5B **12**
Trafalgar Rd. EX8: Lymp 1A **42**
Trafford M. *EX2: Won* 3G **27**
(off Lords Way)
Travershes Cl. EX8: Exmth 6D **42**
Trefusis Pl. EX8: Exmth 4C **48**

Trefusis Ter. EX8: Exmth 4C **48**
Trefusis Way EX9: E Bud 5D **40**
Trelivan Cl. EX8: Exmth 4G **43**
Tremaine Cl. EX14: Hon 3F **23**
Tremford Ct. EX9: Bud S 4F **45**
Trentbridge Sq. EX2: Won 2G **27**
Tresillian Cotts. EX3: Top 5F **33**
Tresillian Gdns. EX3: Top 4F **33**
EX4: Exe 4C **12**
Trevena Cl. EX5: Clyst M 3C **28**
Trews Weir Ct. EX2: Exe 2B **26**
Trews Weir Reach
EX2: Exe 6F **5** (2B **26**)
Triangle, The *EX6: Kenton* 1A **46**
(off Exeter Hill)
EX10: Sidm 6C **38**
Trickhay St. EX4: Exe 3C **4** (6H **11**)
Trinfield Av. EX8: Exmth 6D **42**
Trinity Apartments EX1: Exe 3E **5**
Trinity Ct. EX1: Exe 4E **5** (1A **26**)
EX10: Sidm 6D **38**
Trinity Rd. EX8: Exmth 3A **48**
Tristan Cl. EX4: Whip 2E **13**
Trood La. EX2: Matf 2F **31**
Trow Hill EX10: Sidf 1F **39**
(not continuous)
Trumans Ct. EX4: Exe 5B **4**
Trumps Ct. *EX10: Sidm* 6D **38**
(off East St.)
Truro Dr. EX4: Exe 5E **11**
EX8: Exmth 3F **43**
Trusham Rd. EX2: Mar B 4A **26**
Tucker Rd. EX14: Hon 3E **23**
Tuckers Hall 4B **4** (1H **25**)
Tuckfield Cl. EX2: Won 2E **27**
Tudor Ct. EX4: Exe 4B **4** (1H **25**)
Tudor St. EX4: Exe 4B **4** (1H **25**)
Tuffery Ct. EX4: Exe 4D **12**
Tugela Ter. EX5: Clyst M 3C **28**
Tully Gdns. EX10: Sidm 2D **38**
Tunnel La. EX14: Hon 2H **23**
Tunworth Pl. EX1: Exe 4C **4**
Turkey La. EX5: Rock, Whim 2A **18**
(not continuous)
Turk's Head La. EX14: Hon 4C **22**
Turner Av. EX8: Exmth 2D **48**
Turner Cl. EX10: New P 2D **36**
Turnpike EX14: Hon 4C **22**
Tweed Cl. EX14: Hon 5E **23**
Two Acre Ct. EX2: Alph 6G **25**
Tyrrell Mead EX10: Sidm 2D **38**

U

Ullswater Ct. EX4: Exe 1F **25**
Ulysses Pk. EX2: Sow 1A **28**
Underhill EX8: Lymp 2A **42**
Underhill Cl. EX8: Lymp 3A **42**
Underhill Cres. EX8: Lymp 3A **42**
Underhill Ter. EX3: Top 3F **33**
Unicorn St. EX2: Sow 2H **27**
Union Rd. EX4: Exe 4B **12**
Union St. EX2: Exe 6A **4** (2G **25**)
EX8: Exmth 3C **48**
University of Exeter
Knightley 4H **11**
(off Streatham Dr.)
New North Rd. 5H **11**
Redcot .4H **11**
(off Streatham Dr.)
St Lukes Campus 3G **5** (6B **12**)
Streatham Campus 3H **11**
Upland Chase EX14: Hon 6D **22**
Uplands Dr. EX4: Exe 3E **13**
Upper Barton EX5: Cranb 2A **16**
Up. Church St. EX8: Exmth 3C **48**

Up. Cloister Wlk. *EX6: Exmin* 3H **31**
(off Devington Pk.)
Upper Highfield EX10: Sidm 4C **38**
Up. Paul St. EX4: Exe 2C **4** (6H **11**)
Up. Stoneborough La.
EX9: Bud S 4G **45**
Up. West Ter. EX9: Bud S 4G **45**

V

Vachell Cres. *EX2: Sow* 1H **27**
(off Elliott Way)
Vale Rd. EX8: Exmth 2F **49**
Vales Rd. EX9: Bud S 3H **45**
Valley Pk. Cl. EX4: Exe 2B **12**
Valley Rd. EX4: Exe 5F **11**
EX5: Clyst M 3G **29**
Valley Vw. EX5: Rock 2D **16**
Valley Way EX8: Exmth 4G **43**
Van Buren Pl. EX2: Sow 3H **27**
Vansittart Dr. EX8: Exmth 4E **43**
Varco Sq. EX2: Won 2G **27**
Vaughan Ri. EX1: Whip 6F **13**
Vaughan Rd. EX1: Whip 6F **13**
Veale Dr. EX2: Won 3C **26**
Veitch Cl. EX2: Exe 6H **5** (2C **26**)
Veitch Gdns. EX2: Alph 6H **25**
Velwell Rd. EX4: Exe 1C **4** (5H **11**)
Venn Ottery Rd.
EX10: New P 1B **36**
Venny Bri. EX4: Pin 3H **13**
Verney St. EX1: Exe 1F **5** (5B **12**)
Vernon Rd. EX8: Exmth 5F **43**
Vestry Dr. EX2: Alph 6H **25**
Vicarage Gdns. *EX2: Exe* 2G **25**
(off Old Vicarage Rd.)
Vicarage La. EX4: Pin 2A **14**
Vicarage Rd. EX6: Cockw 3F **47**
EX9: E Bud 5D **40**
EX10: Sidm 5D **38**
Victor Cl. EX1: Heav 1E **27**
Victoria Cl. EX6: Kenton 1A **46**
Victoria Ct. EX4: Exe 4A **4** (1G **25**)
EX8: Exmth 3A **48**
(off Victoria Rd.)
Victoria Pk. Rd. EX2: Exe . . .6H **5** (2C **26**)
Victoria Pl. EX8: Exmth 3C **48**
EX9: Bud S 5G **45**
Victoria Rd. EX3: Top 3F **33**
EX4: Exe 4B **12**
EX8: Exmth 3B **48**
EX10: Sidm 5D **38**
Victoria St. EX4: Exe 4B **12**
Victoria Ter. *EX6: Kennf* 5B **30**
(off Exeter Rd.)
EX11: Ott M 2C **20**
EX14: Hon 3D **22**
(off Dowell St.)
Victoria Way EX8: Exmth 3B **48**
Victoria Yd. EX4: Exe 2C **4** (6H **11**)
Victor La. EX1: Heav 1E **27**
Victor St. EX1: Heav 1E **27**
Victory Ho. EX2: Exe 4E **5**
Vieux Cl. EX9: Ott'n 4G **11**
Village, The EX5: Clyst M 3C **28**
EX5: Rock 3E **17**
Village Cl. EX8: L'ham 2H **49**
Village Rd. EX5: Wood S 1G **35**
Vine Cl. EX2: Exe 5F **5** (1B **26**)
Vine Ho. EX9: Bud S 4H **45**
Vine Pas. *EX14: Hon* 3E **23**
(off Northcote La.)
Vineycroft La. EX10: Sal R 1H **39**
Vision Hill Rd. EX9: Bud S 3H **45**
Vue Cinema
Exeter 2F **5** (6B **12**)

Vuefield Hill EX2: Exe 3E **25**
Vyvyan Ct. *EX1: Heav* *1E 27*
(*off Fore St.*)

W

Wade Cl. EX8: Exmth 1G **49**
Wadham Ho. EX4: Exe 3G **11**
Waggoners Way EX4: Exe 4G **11**
Wagon Hill Way EX2: Won 2D **26**
Wallace Av. EX4: Whip 4F **13**
Walled Garden, The EX2: Cou W 1C **32**
Walls Cl. EX8: Exmth 5F **43**
Walnut Cl. EX6: Exmin 4A **32**
Walnut Gdns. EX4: Exe 1A **4** (5G **11**)
Walnut Gro. EX8: Exmth 2E **49**
Walnut Rd. EX2: Won 4D **26**
EX14: Hon 5C **22**
Walpole Cl. EX4: Whip 3G **13**
Walsingham Pl. EX2: Sow 2H **27**
Walsingham Rd. EX2: Sow 2H **27**
Walton Rd. EX2: Won 1G **27**
Warboro Ter. EX6: Star 1F **47**
Warborough Hill EX6: Kenton 1B **46**
Wardrew Rd. EX4: Exe 1F **25**
Ware Ct. EX14: Hon 5C **22**
Waring Bowen Ct. EX2: Cou W 5D **26**
Warneford Gdns. EX8: Exmth 5G **43**
Warren Cl. EX11: W Hill 5F **19**
Warren Dr. EX9: Bud S 3H **45**
Warren Golf Course **6F 47**
Warren La. EX4: Exe 1E **5** (5A **12**)
Warren Pk. EX11: W Hill 5F **19**
Warrens Mead EX10: Sidf 1F **39**
Warwick Av. EX1: Heav 1G **27**
Warwick Cl. EX14: Fen 1H **9**
Warwick Rd. EX1: Heav 6G **13**
Warwick Way EX4: Whip 4G **13**
Washbrook Vw. EX11: Ott M 1E **21**
Waterbeer St. EX4: Exe 3C **4** (6H **11**)
Waterbridge Ct. EX2: Matf 6B **26**
Watergate EX2: Exe 5D **4** (1A **26**)
Watergate Path *EX2: Exe* *5D 4*
(*off Watergate*)
Watering Ct. EX9: Ott'n 4G **41**
Watering La. EX9: Ott'n 3H **41**
Water La. *EX1: Heav* *1E 27*
(*off Victor La.*)
EX2: Exe 6C **4** (2H **25**)
EX10: Sidm 4D **38**
Waterleat Av. EX14: Hon 4F **23**
Waterloo Rd. EX2: Exe 3G **25**
Watermore Ct. *EX4: Exe* *5C 12*
(*off Pinhoe Rd.*)
Waterside EX2: Exe 6C **4** (2H **25**)
Waterslade La. EX5: Clyst H 4F **15**
Watery La. EX5: Wood 4F **35**
Watson Pl. EX2: Exe 2C **26**
Waverley Av. EX4: Exe 5A **12**
Waverley Rd. EX8: Exmth 1C **48**
Waybrook Cotts. EX2: Matf 1D **30**
Waybrook Cres. EX2: Alph 6H **25**
Waybrook La. EX2: Shil A 2C **30**
Wayland Av. EX2: Exe 6G **5** (2B **26**)
Wayside Cres. EX1: Whip 5F **13**
Wear Barton Rd. EX2: Cou W 6F **27**
Wear Cl. EX2: Cou W 1C **32**
Weatherill Rd. EX14: Hon 6E **23**
Weavers Ct. EX2: Exe 5C **4**
Webbers Caravan & Camping Pk.
EX5: Wood 5H **35**
Webbers Cl. EX5: Whim 4A **8**
Webley Rd. EX2: Exe 3F **25**
Weirfield Ho. EX2: Exe 6E **5**
Weirfield Path EX2: Exe 3B **26**
Weirfield Rd. EX2: Exe 6E **5** (2A **26**)
Weirside Pl. EX2: Exe 6E **5** (2A **26**)
Welcome Family Holiday Pk.
EX7: Daw W 6F **47**
Welcome St. EX2: Exe 2H **25**
Wellington Cl. EX2: Won 1H **27**
Wellington Rd. EX2: Exe 3G **25**
Well Oak Pk. EX2: Won 2D **26**
Wellpark Cl. EX4: Exe 1F **25**
Wells Av. EX14: Fen 1H **9**
Wells Cl. EX8: Exmth 3G **43**
Well St. EX4: Exe 1F **5** (5B **12**)
EX6: Star .1F **47**
Wellswood Gdns. EX4: Exe 1E **25**
Wendover Way EX2: Cou W 4F **27**
Wentworth Gdns. EX4: Exe 2E **25**
Wesley Cl. EX2: Exe 3G **25**
Wesley Way EX2: Alph 6H **25**
Wessex Cl. EX3: Top 2D **32**
Wessex Est. EX4: Exe 4G **11**
West Av. EX4: Exe 4A **12**
Westbourne Ter. EX9: Bud S 5F **45**
Westbrook Cl. EX4: Whip 4F **13**
Westbrook Ct. EX4: Whip 4F **13**
WEST CLYST **1C 14**
W. Clyst Barnyard EX1: W Cly 1D **14**
Westcombe EX2: Alph 6H **25**
Westcott La. EX5: Mar G, Rock 6G **17**
Westcott Way EX14: Hon 3F **23**
W. Down Ct. EX5: Cranb 2B **16**
W. Down La. EX8: L'ham, San B 2H **49**
West End *EX14: Hon* *4D 22*
(*off High St.*)
Western Av. *EX2: Cou W* *1D 32*
(*off Central Av.*)
Western Ct. *EX10: Sidm* *6C 38*
(*off Bedford Sq.*)
Western Dr. EX6: Star 1F **47**
Western Rd. EX4: Exe 4A **4** (1G **25**)
WESTERN TOWN **6C 38**
Western Way EX1: Exe 5B **4** (1H **25**)
(Edmund St.)
EX1: Exe 4E **5** (1A **26**)
(Magdalen St.)
Westfield EX6: Exmin 5B **32**
Westfield Cl. EX9: Bud S 4G **45**
Westfield Gdns. EX9: Bud S 4G **45**
Westfield Rd. EX9: Bud S 4G **45**
West Gth. Ct. EX4: Exe 2F **11**
West Gth. Rd. EX4: Exe 2G **11**
West Gro. Rd. EX2: Exe 6F **5** (1B **26**)
WEST HILL **5F 19**
West Hill EX9: Bud S 4F **45**
West Hill Ct. EX9: Bud S 5F **45**
West Hill Gdns. EX9: Bud S 5F **45**
West Hill La. EX9: Bud S 4F **45**
West Hill Rd. EX11: Ott M, W Hill 6E **19**
Westlands EX8: Exmth 3E **49**
Westminster Cl. EX8: Exmth 4F **43**
EX14: Fen .1H **9**
Westminster Rd. EX4: Exe 6D **10**
WESTON **4A 22**
Weston La. EX14: Awli 2A **22**
Weston Ter. *EX11: Ott M* *1E 21*
(*off Sandhill St.*)
Westown Rd. EX2: Ide 5B **24**
West Pk. Rd. EX10: Sidm 4C **38**
Westpoint Arena **3E 29**
West St. EX1: Exe 4B **4** (1H **25**)
West St. M. EX1: Exe 4B **4**
West Ter. EX1: Heav 6D **12**
EX9: Bud S 4G **45**
Westview Cl. EX5: Whim 4B **8**
West Vw. Ter. EX4: Exe 4B **4** (1H **25**)
EX14: Hon *3D 22*
(*off Dowell St.*)
Westward Dr. EX8: Exmth 2D **48**
WESTWOOD **4E 47**
Westwood Hill EX6: Cockw 3E **47**
Westwood La. EX6: Long 2A **24**
Weycroft Cl. EX1: Sow 6H **13**
Wheat Field La. EX5: Cranb 2A **16**
WHEATLEY **3D 24**
Wheatley Cl. EX4: Exe 1E **25**
Wheatley Ct. EX1: Exe 4C **4**
Wheatsheaf EX5: Cranb 2B **16**
Wheatsheaf Way EX2: Alph 5G **25**
Whiddon La. EX2: Ide 6B **24**
WHIMPLE **4A 8**
Whimple Heritage Cen. **4A 8**
Whimple Station (Rail) **4B 8**
WHIPTON **4F 13**
Whipton Barton Rd. EX1: Whip 5F **13**
Whipton La. EX1: Heav 1E **27**
Whipton Rd. EX4: Whip 4E **13**
Whipton Village Rd.
EX4: Whip 4F **13**
Whitchurch Av. EX2: Won 2F **27**
Whitebeam Cl. EX4: Whip 2F **13**
Whitebridges EX14: Hon 5D **22**
White Cross Rd. EX5: Wood S 2H **35**
White Farm La. EX11: W Hill 6F **19**
Whitefriars Wlk. EX4: Exe 4D **12**
Whitehill La. EX3: Top 6A **28**
White Lodge *EX9: Bud S* *5H 45*
(*off Coastguard Rd.*)
Whiteside Cl. EX2: Won 2G **27**
White Stones EX8: Exmth 3E **49**
White St. EX3: Top 4F **33**
Whitethorn Cl. EX10: Sidm 1B **38**
EX14: Hon 5E **23**
Whitethorn Pk. EX4: Exe 1A **12**
Whiteway Cl. EX5: Whim 4B **8**
Whiteway Dr. EX1: Heav 6F **13**
Whitlow Copse EX2: Won 2G **27**
Whitman Cl. EX8: Exmth 3E **43**
Whitmore Way EX14: Hon 5C **22**
Whitton Ct. EX10: Sidm 2B **38**
Whitycombe Way EX4: Exe 4D **10**
Widecombe Way EX4: Exe 3C **12**
Widgery Rd. EX4: Whip 4E **13**
WIGGATON **5E 21**
Wilcocks Rd. EX4: Pin 3H **13**
Wilford Rd. EX2: Won 1F **27**
Willey's Av. EX2: Exe 6B **4** (2H **25**)
Willeys Ct. EX2: Exe 2H **25**
Williams Av. EX2: Exe 6B **4** (2H **25**)
Willoughby Cl. EX8: Exmth 4E **43**
Willow Av. EX8: Exmth 4D **42**
Willowbrook Av. EX4: Whip 4G **13**
Willow Ct. EX2: Won 2E **27**
Willowdale Cl. EX14: Hon 3D **22**
Willow Gdns. EX5: Broadc 4E **7**
Willows, The EX2: Shil G 4A **30**
Willow Wlk. EX4: Exe 4B **12**
EX14: Hon 5D **22**
Willow Way EX4: Whip 4G **13**
Willsdown Rd. EX2: Alph 6A **26**
Willsland Cl. EX6: Kenton 1A **46**
Wilmot Cl. EX8: Exmth 6G **43**
Wilton Way EX1: Sow 6H **13**
Wiltshier Cl. EX5: Broadc 3E **7**
Wiltshire Cl. EX4: Exe 2E **25**
Winchester Av. EX4: Exe 5E **11**
Winchester Cl. EX14: Fen 1H **9**
Winchester Dr. EX8: Exmth 3F **43**
Windermere Cl. EX4: Exe 6F **11**
Windjammer Ct.
EX8: Exmth 3A **48**
Windmill La. EX11: W Hill 4F **19**
Windrush Ri. EX11: Ott M 2D **20**
Windsor Cl. EX4: Exe 5G **11**
Windsor Dr. EX7: Daw 6C **46**
Windsor Mead EX10: Sidf 1D **38**
Windsor Sq. EX8: Exmth 2C **48**

Windsor Ter. EX6: Kennf 5B 30
(off Exeter Rd.)
Windward Ct. EX8: Exmth 3A 48
Windys Way EX8: Exmth 2F 49
Winkleigh Cl. EX2: Exe 4G 25
Winneford La.
EX14: Awli, Westo 4A 22
Winslade Pk. EX5: Clyst M 5D 28
Winslade Pk. Av. EX5: Clyst M 4C 28
Winslade Rd. EX10: Sidm 3C 38
Winston Rd. EX8: Exmth 4G 43
Winter's La. EX11: Ott M 2D 20
Wish Mdw. La. EX5: Broadc 1F 15
Witcombe La. EX6: Kenton 1A 46
Withalls Gdns. EX8: Lymp 2A 42
Witheby EX10: Sidm 6B 38
Withey, The EX5: Whim 4B 8
Withycombe Pk. Dr. EX8: Exmth . . .5G 43
WITHYCOMBE RALEIGH 6F 43
Withycombe Rd. EX8: Exmth 1C 48
Withycombe Village Rd.
EX8: Exmth 1D 48
WONFORD 2E 27
WONFORD HOUSE HOSPITAL 2D 26
Wonford Rd. EX2: Exe . . .5F 5 (1B 26)
Wonford Sports Cen. 3E 27
Wonford St. EX2: Won 2E 27
Woodah Rd. EX4: Exe 1F 25
Woodbine Ter. EX4: Exe 1B 4 (5H 11)
WOODBURY 5G 35
Woodbury Ct. EX8: Exmth 3E 49
Woodbury Rd. EX3: Clyst G 1A 34
EX5: Wood 2A 34
WOODBURY SALTERTON 1G 35
Woodbury Vw. EX2: Exe 4G 25
EX5: Broadc 4E 7
Woodbury Wlk. EX6: Exmin 3H 31
(off Devington Pk.)
Woodcote Ct. EX5: Wood 5G 35
(off Culvery Cl.)
Woodfield Cl. EX8: Exmth 5G 43
Woodhayes La. EX5: Whim 5B 8
Woodhill Vw. EX14: Hon 6D 22

Woodland M. EX5: Broadc 4F 7
(off Woodland Rd.)
Woodland Rd. EX1: Pin 5H 13
EX5: Broadc 4E 7
Woodlands EX9: Bud S 5E 45
EX10: Sidm 5C 38
Woodlands Ct. EX8: Exmth 4D 42
Woodlands Dr. EX8: Exmth 4D 42
Woodlands Way EX5: Clyst M 3F 29
Wood La. EX8: Exmth 6F 43
Woodleigh Cl. EX4: Exe 1G 11
Woodleys Dr. EX10: New P 1B 36
Woodmans Cres. EX14: Hon 4E 23
Woodside Wlk. EX14: Hon 3F 23
(off Langford Av.)
Woods Pasture EX5: Cranb 2B 16
Woodstock Rd. EX2: Won 1E 27
Woodville Rd. EX2: Exe 3H 25
EX8: Exmth 1C 48
Woodwater La. EX2: Won 2E 27
(not continuous)
Woolaway Av. EX6: Exmin 4B 32
Woolbrook Cl. EX10: Sidm 3C 38
Woolbrook Mead EX10: Sidm 2B 38
Woolbrook Mdws. EX10: Sidm 2C 38
Woolbrook Pk. EX10: Sidm 2C 38
Woolbrook Ri. EX10: Sidm 2C 38
Woolbrook Rd.
EX10: Sidm, Stow 1A 38
Woolcombe La. EX10: Sidm 4D 38
Woolsery Av. EX4: Whip 4F 13
Woolsery Cl. EX4: Whip 4F 13
Woolsery Gro. EX4: Whip 4E 13
Wordsworth Cl. EX8: Exmth 3E 43
World of Country Life, The 6A 44
Wotton Cotts. EX4: Pin 2G 13
Wotton La. EX8: Lymp 2C 42
Wreford's Cl. EX4: Exe 1F 11
Wreford's Dr. EX4: Exe 1G 11
Wreford's La. EX4: Exe 1G 11
Wreford's Link EX4: Exe 1G 11
(not continuous)
Wren Cl. EX14: Hon 5D 22

Wrentham Est. EX4: Exe 4B 12
Wright's La. EX8: Exmth 1H 43
Wykes Rd. EX1: Heav 5D 12
Wynards EX2: Exe 4E 5
Wynards Cl. EX9: E Bud 5D 40
Wynards La. EX2: Exe 4E 5 (1A 26)
Wynards Rd. EX9: E Bud 5D 40
Wyndham Av. EX1: Heav 6D 12
Wynford Rd. EX4: Exe 3D 12

Y

Yallop Way EX14: Hon 5D 22
Yarde Cl. EX10: Sidm 2D 38
Yarde Hill Orchard EX10: Sidm 2D 38
Yardelands EX10: Sidm 2D 38
Yardelands Cl. EX10: Sidm 2D 38
Yarde Mead EX10: Sidm 2D 38
Yeoford Way EX2: Mar B 6B 26
YETTINGTON 3A 40
Yettington Rd. EX9: E Bud 3C 40
Yew Cl. EX14: Hon 5B 22
Yew Tree Cl. EX4: Exe 3C 12
EX8: Exmth 4E 43
Yonder Cl. EX11: Ott M 2E 21
Yonder Cnr. EX11: Ott M 2E 21
(off Chapel La.)
Yonder St. EX11: Ott M 2E 21
York Cl. EX8: Exmth 5G 43
EX14: Fen 1H 9
York Cres. EX14: Fen 1H 9
York Ho. EX4: Exe 1E 5 (5A 12)
York Rd. EX4: Exe 1E 5 (5A 12)
York St. EX10: Sidm 6D 38
(not continuous)
York Ter. EX4: Exe 5B 12
Younghayes Rd. EX5: Cranb 3A 16

Z

Zig Zag Path EX9: Bud S 5F 45

The representation on the maps of a road, track or footpath is no evidence of the existence of a right of way.

The Grid on this map is the National Grid taken from Ordnance Survey® mapping with the permission of the Controller of Her Majesty's Stationery Office.

SAFETY CAMERA INFORMATION

PocketGPSWorld.com's CamerAlert is a self-contained speed and red light camera warning system for SatNavs and Android or Apple iOS smartphones/tablets. Visit www.cameralert.co.uk to download.

Safety camera locations are publicised by the Safer Roads Partnership which operates them in order to encourage drivers to comply with speed limits at these sites. It is the driver's absolute responsibility to be aware of and to adhere to speed limits at all times.

By showing this safety camera information it is the intention of Geographers' A-Z Map Company Ltd., to encourage safe driving and greater awareness of speed limits and vehicle speed. Data accurate at time of printing.

Printed and bound in the United Kingdom by Gemini Press Ltd., Shoreham-by-Sea, West Sussex
Printed on materials from a sustainable source